Houseplant Style

Houseplant Style

Creative ideas for decorating your home

SUSAN CONDER

Michael O'Mara Books Limited

First published in 1993 by Michael O'Mara Books Limited,
9 Lion Yard, Tremadoc Road, London SW4 7NQ

Houseplant Style copyright © Susan Conder 1993

A CIP catalogue record for this book is available from the British Library

ISBN 1-85479-139-7 (hardback)
ISBN 1-85479-961-4 (paperback)

Designed by Jeanette Collins
Typeset by Florencetype Ltd, Kewstoke, Avon
Printed and bound in Italy by Amilcare Pizzi

Contents

Acknowledgments

The publishers are grateful to the following for permission to reproduce illustrations:
(where names are given, the photographer is credited first, followed by the stylist)

Copyright © La Maison de Marie Claire: pp. 20–21, Duard/Puech; pp. 22–23, Briand/Comte;
pp. 28–29, Hussenot/Puech; pp. 32–33, Galland/Pellé; p. 34, Chabaneix/Sédillot-Postic; p. 36, Pataut/Bayle, Puech;
p. 63, Hussenot/Comte; p. 68, 102, Pataut/Bayle; p. 73, Hussenot/Faver; p. 83, 110, Rozés/Hirsh-Marie; p. 89,
Pliabo-Godeaut/Realis, Bayle; p. 92, Girardeau/Postic; p. 99, Pataut/Puech; p. 101, Pataut/Comte;
p. 103, Hussenot/La Motte

Copyright © 100 idées: p. 12, 26–27, 47, 51, 81, 87, 106, Maltaverne/Faver; p. 107, Maclean/LeBeau;
pp. 54, 55, 67, Laiter

Elle Decoration: p. 14–15, June Buck/Domenica More Gordon; p. 25 Christophe Kicherer; p. 30–31,
Mike Parsons/Domenica More Gordon; p. 39, James Merrell/Karina Garrick, Kate Constable; p. 41,
James Merrell/Barbara Hajek, Claire Heseltine; p. 91, James Mortimer/room design by Anthony Collett and David
Champion; p. 96, Simon Wheeler/Domenica More Gordon; p. 105, Bill Batten/Jane Cumberbatch

EWA: pp. 5, 8, 18–19, 35, 37, 38, 44–45, 46, 48, 49, 57, 61, 62, 66, 74–5, 76, 77, 79, 80, 82–3 (left),
85, 88, 90, 94, 95, 97, 100, 109, 112–113, 114, 115, 116, 125

Photographs by Linda Burgess: pp. 6–7, 10–11, 16–17, 42–43

Robert Harding Picture Library: pp. 60, Brian Harrison; p. 71, © IPC Magazines: Simon Page-Ritchie;
p. 98, Spike Powell; p. 119, Christopher Drake; 120, Mike Newton

Derrick Witty: pp. 52, 53, 70, 107 (right)

Moggy: pp. 58–59, 84, 117

Pictures for pp. 64–65, 122, courtesy of Marston & Langinger Conservatories,
192 Ebury Street, London, SW1W 8UP, telephone: 071 824 8818

Introduction

Attitudes change all the time towards all sorts of things – politics, fashion, fidelity and diet, to name a few – and attitudes towards houseplants are no exception. Formerly, buying and looking after houseplants was a serious, almost moral, business and books on houseplants reflected this *in loco parentis* concern and responsibility for their well-being. Raising the perfect houseplant, like raising the perfect child, was the ultimate goal. Books included many obscure and difficult species, and weighty sections on propagation, potting compost and dealing with pests, diseases and other afflictions.

Houseplant Style is different. It acknowledges that, now, the vast majority of houseplants are bought by people who see them primarily as decorative objects and secondly as living things. Most people simply want to buy their plant in perfect condition from a convenient local source, and display it to best advantage. Though they're prepared to look after a plant within reason, if anything goes drastically wrong, they dispose of it and buy a new one. Quick gratification has replaced painstaking commitment and *Houseplant Style* is written to reflect, and indeed, to celebrate, this new approach.

Equal weight is given to plants and style, that is, grouping and displaying them to achieve the maximum visual impact. Creative propping, long the preserve of the professional stylist and interior decorator, is an easy, often cheap, way to transform even the most mundane spider plant or aspidistra into a charming focal point. As a creative catalogue, *Houseplant Style* encourages an adventurous approach by providing masses of ideas for traditional and unusual plant combinations, containers and settings.

Whatever your chosen decor – Victorian, Mediterranean, country cottage or American, *Houseplant Style* will show you how to make your houseplants emphasize this. At the same time, the room by room guide will help you to choose the plants which are most suitable for the surrounding conditions, as well as those which best complement a room's particular function. There are also ideas for festive themes, from making a potted cyclamen 'say' Christmas by displaying it in a holly wreath, to complicated centrepieces for the dining table.

Combining cut flowers and houseplants, the traditional *pot et fleur* display, is revisited with a fresh eye, with many suggested combinations for bringing temporary flower colour and fragrance to houseplants, at the same time as providing cut flowers with more interesting foliage than the predictable sprig of florists' cypress or asparagus fern.

Photographs in this book stress the plants' setting rather than simply showing mug shots, with full frontals and profiles of plants against plain backgrounds, as if newly arrested. Relaxed and visually seductive, *Houseplant Style* sets the style for a whole new generation of houseplant books.

9

The Plants

Short-term Houseplants

SOME HOUSEPLANTS SHOULD be considered as cut flowers that happen to have roots and are disposed of once past their best just like faded cut flowers are, without feelings of guilt or extravagance. Some are annuals that die naturally after flowering; virtually any garden annual can be treated as a short-term houseplant. Others are hardy or tender bulbs, shrubs or perennials that require careful management, often including periods of dormancy and/or spells outdoors, if they are to flower again indoors; there are many books dealing with detailed aspects of plant care, if you are interested.

Most short-term houseplants are grown for their colourful blooms; potted chrysanthemums, for example, polyanthus (*Primula polyanthus* hybrids) and busy Lizzies (*Impatiens wallerana* hybrids). The newest and very popular is the miniature rose 'houseplant' (*Rosa chinensis minima* hybrids). A few, such as coleus (*Coleus blumei* hybrids), are grown for their leaves or, with winter cherry (*Solanum capsicastrum*), for their berries.

These are the ideal impulse-buy plants – like a cheap pair of earrings or brief fling, it's not a long-term investment or commitment – and you can be imaginative, even outrageous, in choice. Often they are sold at a discount if you buy several and flower market stalls, at the end of the day, may sell them for ridiculously low prices, so you can create considerable impact for little outlay, by filling a wicker

The long and short of it

Cyclamen, among the most popular and common houseplants in autumn and winter, have a potential lifespan far longer than is often realized. Though usually discarded after flowering (and often killed by too much watering, direct sunlight and excessive heat), they can flower year after year, increasing in number of flowers, if properly treated.

After flowering, gradually reduce feeding and watering, then when bone dry place the plant, its pot turned on its side, in a cool, shady spot until midsummer. Re-pot using fresh compost, and reverse the process, gradually increasing food and water, as growth gets underway. Bring under cover well before frost threatens.

basket or soup tureen with several, for example, or displaying them in a row on a window-sill or interspersed among books on a shelf – formal repetition is always powerful. Use them to add new interest to a group of permanent, floor-level foliage plants, perhaps placing them on a little table or stand, so that they seem to hover above the greenery.

Follow the instructions on the care label –

most are Temperate-climate plants that like cool, bright, airy surroundings – but if you want to display them in inhospitable conditions, it only foreshortens what is an inevitable conclusion, anyway. Unfortunately, not all ephemeral plants are cheap; arum lilies (*Zantedeschia aethiopica*), azaleas (*Rhododendron simsii* hybrids), hydrangeas (*Hydrangea macrophylla*) and even poinsettias (*Euphorbia pulcher-*

Greener grass

Any seed capable of germination is fair game as a potential short-lived houseplant. Here, wheat, barley and other grains, members of the *Gramineae*, or grass, family and normally grown for strictly practical reasons, become indoor ornaments.

Such grains sprout easily, given warmth and rich, moist soil, and hold fascination for children and adults alike. Lush, grassy growth such as this is a symbol of renewal – indeed, sprouting grains in special receptacles formed part of Ancient Egyptian seasonal religious rituals – and the start of the mowing season for lawn owners. When past its best, this display can be discarded or placed on the compost heap, and the containers used for the next short-term display, such as primroses dug up from the garden and enlivened with cut stems of red-barked dogwood.

rima) can be costly, especially if medium-sized or large specimens. And crotons (*Codiaeum variegatum pictum*) and gardenias (*Gardenia jasminoides*), with their need for continual heat and humidity, are usually short-lived.

Because they have an 'enjoy by' date, try to site ephemeral plants in prominent positions. You can repeat their 'here-today, gone-tomorrow' quality in the choice of container,

perhaps wrapping the plastic pot in brightly coloured tissue paper, gift wrapping paper or even foil, splayed out at the top and tied with a ribbon. Try to conceal plastic pots, however, even if it just means slipping them, pot and all, into a terracotta pot or into the top of an attractive jug or pitcher, propping up the pot on crumpled newspaper, if necessary, and covering the surface of the potting compost with moss.

TIP

Pots of polyanthus or early tulips (*Tulipa greigii* hybrids) bought from a garden centre are often cheaper than from a florist, and if you can buy them in a tray or flat and pot them up yourself, they are cheaper still.

SHORT-TERM PLANTS
Arum lily (*Zantedeschia aethiopica*)
Azalea (*Rhododendron simsii* hybrids)
Basket begonia (*Begonia pendula* hybrids)
Bead plant (*Nertera depressa*)
Black-eyed Susan (*Thunbergia alata*)
Caladium (*Caladium hortulanum* hybrids)
Cape Heath (*Erica* species)
Christmas pepper (*Capsicum annuum*)
Chrysanthemum (*Chrysanthemum morifolium* hybrids)
Cineraria (*Senecio cruentus*)
Coleus (*Coleus blumei* hybrids)
Cupid's bower (*Achimines hybrida*)
Cyclamen (*Cyclamen persicum* varieties)
Genista (*Cytisus racemosus*)
Gloxinia (*Sinningia speciosa* hybrids)
Hydrangea (*Hydrangea macrophylla* varieties)
Persian violet (*Exacum affine*)
Poinsettia (*Euphorbia pulcherrima*)
Polyanthus (*Primula polyanthus* hybrids)
Poor man's orchid (*Schizanthus* x *hybrida*)
Rose (*Rosa chinensis minima* hybrids)
Slipper flower (*Calceolaria herbeohybrida*)
Tuberous rooted begonia (*Begonia tuberhybrida*)
Winter cherry (*Solanum capsicastrum*)

13

Flower versus Foliage

This is a hypothetical contest, since all flowering houseplants have leaves and except for ferns and mosses, all houseplants have the potential to flower, though many fail to in the alien environment of a home. Others that flower – coleus (*Coleus blumei* hybrids), for example, or umbrella plant (*Cyperus alternifolius*) – produce insignificant blooms; coleus flower buds are actually nipped out to keep

the plant compact and the leaves fresh looking. The most popular flowering houseplants are generally those that produce large, showy, colourful blooms, ranging from cheap and cheerful tuberous-rooted begonias (*Begonia tuberhybrida*) and pelargoniums (*Pelargonium hortorum* hybrids) to exotic orchids.

As well as the attraction of colour, there is the symbolic aspect: roses are symbols of love, lilies of purity, forced hyacinths and 'Paperwhite' narcissi of spring. Flowers being reproductive organs also convey sexuality, whether the feminine delicacy of dipladenia (*Dipladenia sanderi* 'Rosea') or the frankly phallic form of peace lily or white sails spathes

(*Spathiphyllum wallisii*). Flowers are also valued for their relatively short lives and intimations of self-indulgence and extravagance; probably more flowering than foliage houseplants are impulse buys!

The visual distinction between flowers and foliage is, in some cases, blurred. The bright red, pink or white 'flowers' of poinsettias are actually coloured, leaf-like bracts, as are the showy pink, blue or mauve 'flowers' of hydrangeas, the brilliant red 'flowers' of flaming sword (*Vriesia splendens*) and the bright pink 'flowers' of the paper flower (*Bougainvillea glabra*).

In terms of colour, the leaves of plants such

Living geometry

Pliable or prunable foliage plants, without the distraction of gaudy flowers, present the raw material for living sculptures. Those such as ivy, box and bay, with dense growth habit, are ideal.

Here (from the left), a pair of clipped dwarf box balls and a smaller pair of naturally globe-shaped mind-your-own-business flank an ivy, trained to form a quartered globe; clipped box spirals and tiny lavenders flank a miniature standard bay.

In their white pots and set against a white background, the foliage plants display their subtle differences – differences that might otherwise be lost in the normal hurly burly of domestic decor.

15

as rex begonia (*Begonia rex* hybrids), coleus (*Coleus blumei* hybrids), crotons (*Codiaeum variegatum pictum* hybrids) and angel's wings (*Caladium hortulanum* hybrids) are as colourful as any flower, displaying the high-key hues of their tropical origins. The leaves of blushing bromeliad (*Neoregelia carolinae* 'Tricolor') actually form a flower-like rosette, the centre of which turns clear red as the insignificant flowers develop.

In terms of restfulness, green foliage is most effective. The variation in leaf shape, size and surface texture, and in the different tints and shades of green, offer opportunity for subtle contrast. Green is never 'just' green! If restful flowers are desired, choose white or green blooms – green-flowering tobacco plants, for example or green arum lilies (*Zantedeschia aethiopica* 'Green Goddess').

In terms of permanence, leaves give more value for money, with few exceptions being evergreen, and in terms of scale, the largest leaf is much larger than the largest flower. Some houseplants such as queen's tears (*Billbergia nutans*) do combine attractive foliage with reliable, long-lasting flowers; for the others, it is a question of enjoying the foliage alone, juxtaposing flowering and foliage houseplants or resorting to combining fake flowers with foliage houseplants – not at all dishonorable!

Colour and pattern

Leaves can be as colourful as flowers, and with their longer natural lives, even if deciduous, repay any space and care given them. Green and white is a common combination, here represented by the goosefoot plant, *Syngonium podophyllum*, and the tiny, white-veined silver net leaf, *Fittonia argyroneura*.

Begonia rex varieties – two are shown – could form the basis of a collection, so varied are their exotic colourations and patterns. The rich fuchsia and maroon polka dot plant (*Hypoestes sanguinolenta*) repeats the exotic colour theme in its little leaves, and lastly, the poinsettia 'flowers', actually leaf-like bracts, show how pointless the hard division between flower and foliage plant is.

Friendly and familiar

Weeping figs are almost as much a fixture as televisions in living rooms, but with their long-lived tolerance of less than perfect care and normal domestic temperatures, their popularity is understandable.

They also have the quality of being able to fit virtually any decor – like chameleons, but without the colour change, they absorb the quality of their surroundings.

There are now several coloured-leaved forms, as well as the white-edged 'Variegata', including 'Starlight', 'Gold Princess' and 'Hawaii', but the green-leaved species is the most widely available.

Be careful of overwatering weeping figs; let the compost dry out a bit between waterings. Provide protection from fierce sunlight, feed them in spring and summer, dust them occasionally, and let them get on with it.

Long-term Plants

The cost, size, ease of cultivation and potential longevity of houseplants are often, but not always, interrelated and all affect the definition of 'long-term'. With the cost of large specimen houseplants running into high double or even triple figures, such plants are usually expected to last for years in normal domestic conditions. Palms such as Kentia palm and sentry palm (*Howea* species), weeping figs (*Ficus benjamina*), umbrella trees (*Schefflera actinophylla*), tree philodendrons (*Philodendron selloum, P. bipinnatifidum*), Madagascar dragon trees (*Dracaena marginata*) and clivias (*Clivia miniata*), given reasonable treatment, are likely to stay the course.

Other costly houseplants – orange and lemon trees (*Citrus* species) in fruit, for example, or gardenias (*Gardenia jasminoides*) in flower – are difficult. You are paying for the show which in warm, dry conditions is short-lived, and are left with awkward plants afterwards. The lovely and currently fashionable house lime or Zimmer linden (*Sparmannia africana*) offers no such obvious lure but needs cooler winter conditions and more humid summer ones than ordinary, centrally heated homes can provide. Before buying, always ask about the needs and ease of cultivation of a houseplant, especially if costly, that you see as a long-term investment.

On the other hand, inexpensive rubber plants (*Ficus elastica* varieties) and Swiss cheese plants (*Monstera deliciosa*) can go on virtually for ever and, unlike most specimen houseplants, can grow quite substantially given ordinary care and conditions. Somehow, larger plants do tend to be considered longer-term investments than smaller ones, though the cast-iron plant (*Aspidistra elatior*) and

19

mother-in-law's tongue (*Sansevieria* species and varieties) are modest sized but with very strong survival instincts. And cacti can live for a hundred years or more, increasing in size imperceptibly from one decade to the next. Small, young cacti are cheap and even medium-sized plants tend to be reasonably priced, unless in flower – flowering puts the price up at a stroke.

Taken in the broader sense, long term can be viewed generationally; any houseplant that reproduces quickly and easily provides a potentially infinite number of replacements. The children, grandchildren and great grand-children of a single spider plant (*Chlorophytum comosum* 'Vittatum'), piggyback plant (*Tolmeia menziesii*), cyperus (*Cyperus species*) or African violet (*Saintpaulia ionantha* hybrids), for example, can fill a room or, eventually, whole home with verdure. And finally, stretching a point, short-term houseplants such as minia-ture roses, hydrangeas and chrysanthemums can become long-term garden plants, hard-ened off and planted out after flowering.

Double design statement

Two pairs of sculptural, twisted-stemmed yuccas, each comprising a taller and shorter plant, empha-size the decor's sharp form and symmetry, mirrored also in the arrangement of the four chairs.

A sense of timelessness is reflected in the choice of plants – yuccas and the fat round cacti in the corner are very slow growing – and the picture of the pyramids that takes pride of place on the wall.

Yuccas and cacti both benefit from a spell in a sunny garden in summer, and a cool, sunny spot indoors, especially in winter. Both require minimum watering in winter, the barest drop from time to time, and liberal supplies in spring and summer.

The peachy tulips add a colourful, frivolous note: a 'here today, gone tomor-row' touch that counter-acts the room's sobriety.

Exotica

Exotic literally means introduced from abroad but since many common houseplants and garden plants originally came from abroad – tulips, for example, from Turkey, lilies from the Orient and Eastern Europe and cyclamen from Mediterranean regions – in the context of houseplant style, exotic usually refers to the strikingly attractive colour, large size and unusual, even curious, form of the flowers. Exotic also hints at extravagance, since exotics were originally costly status symbols; of rarity value, since mass-market plants lose their exclusivity; and of challenge, since exotics can be temperamental. Optimum growing conditions vary, but tropical and subtropical jungles of Africa, India and South America, with constant heat and humidity, are the source of many exotics.

The gaudy appearance, and often heady scent, of exotic flowers evolved to attract pollinators. Typical are tropical orchids, with their delicate markings serving as nectar guides to bees, wasps or moths, or in some cases, mimicking a female of the pollinating species, to attract a male to mate (and pollinate) under false pretenses!

Other exotics include the bird-of-paradise flower (*Strelitzia reginae*), with its beak-like 'landing pad' for birds and orange and blue flowers; the so-called orchid cactus (*Epiphyllum ackermanii, E. cooperi* hybrids), a forest cactus with an ungainly growth habit but brilliant red, yellow, orange, pink or white blooms up to 15 cm (6 in across); bromeliads such as the blue-flowered torch (*Tillandsia lindenii*), with flattened, paddle-like pink flower bracts and blue flowers; columneas (*Columnea* species), hanging plants covered with brilliant orange, lipped blooms; and the glory lily (*Gloriosa rothschildiana*), a climber with orange and yellow lily-like blooms. Definitely difficult but fantastic are angel's

trumpet (*Datura* species and varieties), with enormous, richly scented, pendant white, yellow or orange trumpet blooms, and rose grape (*Medinella magnifica*), with huge, hanging, tiered pink blooms.

Exotic foliage plants include the curious elephant foot or ponytail plant (*Beaucarnia recurvata*) with bulb-like woody base topped by a pony tail rosette of leaves, and the black-gold philodendron (*Philodendron melanochrysum*), with velvety, almost black leaves.

In style terms, if you have exotics, flaunt them, in the same way that they flaunt themselves for pollinators. An exotic setting helps emphasize their specialness. The container could be reminiscent of the source, such as rough African or blue and white Persian pottery; repeat the main flower colour in glazed ceramic. For epiphytic exotics, such as bromeliads and many orchids, that normally live on trees, bird's-nest-like baskets of moss and twigs add a naturalistic touch.

Stage setting

Most houseplants are exotic, in the technical sense that they aren't native, but some look decidedly more exotic than others. Then, too, an exotic decor such as this one can convince the eye that even the most mundane native plants are somehow tropical or at least unusual.

Here, a pair of palm trees, a bonsai and bamboo represent plant environments ranging from temperate to tropical, and horticultural approaches which range from the minimal intervention needed in caring for palms to the highly artificial, extremely skilled and symbolic craft of bonsai.

A sense of mystery

Orchidaceae, the orchid family, includes modest, temperate–climate terrestrial species as well as flamboyant, tropical ones but the name itself is enough to conjure up images of the exotic.

In this almost unreal setting, various tropical orchids look right at home. *Cymbidiums*, the most commonly and easily grown orchid houseplant, flank the chair, with flat-faced, pink moth orchids (*Phalaenopsis* hybrids), at floor level and attached to poles, mimicking their natural, epiphytic growth habit.

Spanish moss (*Tillandsia usneoides*), a bromeliad, cascades from the poles and statue's outstretched hand, much as it does from tree branches in its native American swamps.

The statue also holds a *Paphiopedilum* (syn. *Cypripedium*) hybrid, or slipper orchid, so called from its pouch-like lower lip. It merits pride of place since the flowers of this terrestrial tropical orchid can last two to three months; another is displayed on the side table, together with a speckled and spotted, extravagant *Odontoglossum* cross.

Miniatures

An object or living thing complete in all its parts but diminutive in scale has timeless fascination and appeal: tiny china figurines, for example, new-born babies, miniature poodles and, of course, tiny houseplants. Houseplants can be temporarily or permanently miniature: little rooted cuttings of variegated ivy (*Hedera helix* 'Glacier'), for example, can soon outgrow the category; slow-growing cacti may remain small for years, but eventually become substantial; while dwarf sports of larger plants such as the miniature pomegranate (*Punica granatum* 'Nana') and micro-miniature African violets remain permanently small.

Houseplants can be given a helping hand in remaining tiny, by various combinations of restrictive potting, feeding, training and pruning. Topiary and bonsai techniques, for example, can be applied to houseplants such as weeping fig (*Ficus benjamina*), Buddhist pine (*Podocarpus macrophyllus*), false holly (*Osmanthus heterophyllus* 'Variegatus') and azalea (*Rhododendron simsii* hybrids). More easily, you can make 'instant' miniature houseplants by removing a few stems from a large old peanut cactus (*Chamaecereus sylvestri*) and re-planting them, or potting up the plantlets of spider plant (*Chlorophytum comosum* 'Vittatum') or mother-of-thousands (*Saxifraga stolonifera* 'Tricolor') in tiny pots. Carpet-forming houseplants such as the bead plant (*Nertera depressa*), mind-your-own-business (*Soleirolia soleirolii*) or various selaginellas (*Selaginella* species and varieties) can simply be divided and the sections replanted in smaller pots.

Though tiny plants are often cheaper than large plants – 'tots' sold at garden centres and florists' shops, for example – newly developed dwarf varieties and those that require ongoing labour to remain small (such as bonsai), can be

remarkably expensive, given their small size.

As with displaying tiny figurines, displaying tiny plants requires thought and immaculate, safe settings. Grouping them in dish gardens, tray gardens, terrariums or bottle gardens (see pages 50–51) provides protection from accidental knocks and being forgotten altogether, often the fate of miniature plants displayed singly. Individual miniature plants can

Another world

Miniature gardens can be as rewarding as full-scale ones, to those with a certain type of mind – not only children are fascinated by the diminutive.

This is a frankly short-term ensemble, since the ferns, mosses and *Selaginella* thrive in cool, indirectly lit, humid conditions, the exact opposite of the succulent, sun-loving houseleeks, waterfall-like strings of beads, *Senecio rowleyanus*, and fuchsia-flowered succulent in the fore-ground. None the less, it can give several weeks' pleasure before being disassembled.

The large, porous rock, the white chippings and the tiny, toothpick 'bridge' allude to a landscape, without becoming too literal or twee.

be charming, however, in a container that adds visual and actual weight to their pres-ence: a small ceramic cherub carrying a basket containing a trailing miniature ivy, for exam-ple; an old-fashioned printer's wooden type-face box with a miniature plant in each compartment; or more humorously, an open-topped model car sporting a miniature plant in the passenger seat. And although mirrors have tremendous impact reflecting huge houseplants, they can be equally valuable reflecting the image of a miniature plant, as if reflecting a precious jewel.

TIP
Miniature plants displayed singly dry out quickly, so check every couple of days and water as necessary.

Total Fakes

There is nothing morally or even aesthetically wrong with artificial houseplants and they can often give a great deal of pleasure in an environment hostile to live ones. Windowless bathrooms or halls, for example, can be enhanced with them, as can windowsills above radiators – a fatal location for many houseplants – or dark, draughty landings. Even an environment perfect for houseplants need not be discounted, especially if you aren't green fingered. The mantelpiece above a living-room fireplace, for example, is far better served with a magnificent pair of fake plants than ailing live ones.

KEYS TO SUCCESS

Part of the difference between success and failure is one of attitude: humorously or dramatically placed fake houseplants often succeed in pleasing, where a similar plant, displayed in an ill-considered or half-hearted way, can present a double disappointment. The more opulent the decor, the less likely the mind's eye to perceive and criticize the fraud, rather like a rhinestone pin on a real mink coat, or a diamond pin on a fake mink coat.

The other major factor is the quality of the houseplant itself. They can be realistic or frankly fake, but a poor quality realistic one, which doesn't quite convince, can be worse than none at all. Poor quality realistic ones set in plastic 'potting compost' represent the nadir of houseplant style and, if worth saving, are best transferred to terracotta or other containers and anchored in peat-based potting compost, or the plastic 'potting compost' covered with a decorative mulch (see pages 66–67). The one exception is really poor-quality fake houseplants chosen and displayed as totally kitsch objects, perhaps in the plastic and vinyl setting of '50s decor, complete, perhaps, with kidney-shaped coffee table.

MIX, MATCH AND MOVE

In the same way as for *pot et fleur*, fresh flowers or foliage and fake houseplants can be combined, or fake and live houseplants, the latter giving an air of authenticity to the former. Thick, fleshy *cymbidium* sprays, for example, are sold singly because of their cost, but don't mix well with other blooms and can look odd on their own. Fronted by a fake Boston fern, each adds interest to the other, however unlikely the

Gutsy

Like dyed blonde hair, the most successful examples of fake plants are often those which are top quality, or those which proclaim their fraudulence, rather than attempt in a half-hearted way to conceal it.

Here, a fake weeping fig fills a dark corner, joining forces with a real ivy to soften visually the hard geometry of furniture, floor, walls and artwork.

combination botanically. A magnolia branch in bloom, cut from the garden, could be similarly displayed. Moving fake houseplants around from time to time helps prevent their being taken for granted, in the same way that an artificial flower arrangement, left long in the same place, becomes virtually invisible to the daily beholder.

You can display fake plants in groups as well as singly. High-level displays of fake climbing plants can be great fun, and because you can't inspect them up close, the effect can be very nearly real.

Dust or wash long-term fake houseplants from time to time, to keep them fresh looking; any that have faded from long exposure to sun can be sprayed silver, gold, copper or bronze and used in Christmas displays. A houseplant going through a temporary bad patch can be camouflaged with fake ivy trails, twining up its bare stem or in its branches.

Herbs

No one expects herbs to make a striking impression, even at the best of times. Popular garden herbs such as parsley, sage, thyme and rosemary have modest, if any, floral impact but are valued for their rich history, aromatic foliage, appeal to bees and butterflies and culinary use. As short-term kitchen house-plants, however, herbs rarely have to compete with gaudier subjects and there is something comforting about their presence.

Space is a natural limitation, excluding larger herbs such as angelica. Compact ornamental varieties such as purple-leaved basil (*Ocimum basilicum* 'Dark Opal') and variegated lemon balm (*Melissa officinalis* 'Variegata') are fun and provide the same aroma as the plain-leaved counterparts. Buy several of one type and plant close together in a single container or plant variations on a theme – in purple-, yellow- and multi-coloured variegated sage, for example. They look better than single plants and you can pick sprigs regularly without denuding any one plant.

Line herbs out on a windowsill or shelves fixed across the window or place them, one above another, in brackets fixed vertically to the reveals, like a herbal apartment house! Use traditional terracotta herb pots or parsley pots or decorative containers, perhaps featuring images or calligraphic representations of the herbs they contain. Brightly coloured plastic pots are in keeping with the humble quality of herbs, and practical in a kitchen, or use pretty Italian tomato tins, emptied washed, then varnished and perforated at the bottom for drainage.

30

Books on herb growing are always quick to point out that, compared to other ornamental garden plants, many herbs are dull-looking, with small flowers and undramatic leaves.

Taken as a challenge, displaying herbs indoors can be a flamboyant and creative exercise. Here, (from the left) twiggy pots contain little thyme bushes surrounded by spring onions, either side of a painted, twine-wrapped and moss-adorned wooden crate garden filled with parsley, young sweetcorn and cut dogwood branches, which might well root while being displayed, and can then be planted in the garden.

The wacky, slightly surreal, wire-mesh netting flowerpots and urn hold mustard and cress, chives and dogwood branches, and a red-leaf lettuce, respectively.

Alternatively, make a complete herb garden in miniature in an indoor window box, large alpine pan or planting trough – well drained, not too rich potting compost and plenty of drainage material at the base. (You can use the alpine pan herb garden as an instant table centrepiece, perhaps with a pair of tiny scissors, so diners can help themselves to fresh herbs.)

Maximum light (less so for mint) and ventilation and, in winter, cool conditions are best. Though their natural association is with the kitchen, herbs also thrive in a cool conservatory. When herbs begin to look jaded, plant in the garden or discard and replace with fresh. If you grow herbs permanently outdoors, create a herb rota, bringing a selection in, enjoying them, returning them to the garden to recover and potting up vigorous replacements. Herbs are especially useful indoors from autumn until spring; tender herbs such as basil, normally killed by frost, repay being brought indoors in autumn with weeks or months of fresh leaves.

HERBS TO GROW
Basil (*Ocimum* species and varieties)
Chervil (*Anthriscus cerefolium*)
Chives (*Allium schoenoprasum*)
Lemon balm (*Melissa officinalis*)
Marjoram (*Origanum majorana*)
Mint (*Mentha* species and varieties)
Parsley (*Petroselinium crispum*)
Rosemary (*Rosmarinus officinalis*)
Sage (*Salvia officinalis* species and varieties)
Summer savory (*Satureja hortensis*)
Thyme (*Thymus* species and varieties)
Winter savory (*Satureja montana*)

The Roles

Focal Point Plants

HOUSEPLANTS OFTEN ACT as focal points by virtue of their size but siting and setting are equally important. Large, impressive, floor-standing houseplants with strong architectural form – huge leaves, for example, arching branches or sinuous trunks – are natural choices and the larger the better, in terms of instant impact. (Always buy the biggest focal-point plant you can afford for floor-standing displays; few grow substantially or rapidly except in tropical or very controlled commercial greenhouse conditions.) Large cacti and curiosities such as the ponytail plant, (*Beaucarnea recurvata*) and *Jatropha podagrica* with their huge, swollen root base, make good focal points because of their strongly sculptural character.

Like sculptures in a museum, focal point plants command attention in relation to the surroundings; the more empty, neutral space around them, the more the plant's visual importance is confirmed. Museums play the trick to extremes, displaying a single, even quite small, sculpture in a vast empty gallery. Though this option is rarely available on the domestic front, substantial, neutral space around a large plant helps add to its power, as does dramatic lighting, complete with shadows. In a room with heavily patterned wallpaper, a plain painted panel behind a plant adds to its impact.

Smaller, individual plants can also act as focal points by virtue of their position – an African violet (*Saintpaulia ionantha* hybrid) placed in the middle of a dining-room table, for example, is as powerful a focal point as a large, free-standing plant. And just like a pulpit or rostrum elevates a speaker, literally and symbolically, a Boston fern (*Nephrolepis exaltata* 'Bostoniensis') on a wooden, marble or faux-marble plinth is likewise imbued with extra 'pulling' power.

Contrasting colour can contribute to a small plant's visual impact: the all-white, minimalist rooms of the '60s often featured one red hippeastrum (*Hippeastrum* hybrids) or flamingo flower (*Anthurium scherzeranum*) – focal points in spite of their modest size.

A larger-than-life tin can holds a dwarf banana tree, a powerful focal point by dint of its size, its corner position and the museum-like white and neutral surroundings. The raised cacti garden along the side wall benefits from the skylight directly above.

LARGE FOCAL POINT PLANTS
African hemp (*Sparmannia africana*)
Areca palm (*Chrysalidocarpus lutescens*)
Bamboo palm (*Chamaedorea erumpens*)
Benghal fig (*Ficus benghalensis*)
Canary date palm (*Phoenix canariensis*)
Chinese fan palm (*Livistona chinensis*)
Corn palm (*Dracaena fragrans*)
European fan palm (*Chamaerops humilis*)
False castor oil plant (*Fatsia japonica*)
Fiddle-leaf fig (*Ficus lyrata*)
Kangaroo vine (*Cissus antarctica*)
Kentia palm (*Howea fosteriana*)
Lady palm (*Rhapis excelsa*)

Madagascar dragon tree (*Dracaena marginata*)
Parasol plant (*Heptapleurum arboricola*)
Parlour palm (*Chamaedorea elegans*)
Ponytail plant (*Beaucarnea recurvata*)
Reed palm (*Chamaedorea seifrizii*)
Rubber plant (*Ficus elastica*)
Spanish bayonet (*Yucca aloifolia*)
Spineless yucca (*Y. elephantipes*)
Swiss-cheese plant (*Monstera deliciosa*)
Tree philodendron (*Philodendron bipinnatifidum*)
Umbrella tree (*Schefflera actinophylla*)
Weeping fig (*Ficus benjamina*)
Windmill palm (*Trachycarpus fortunei*)

33

Houseplants as Wallpaper

Plants, in time, naturally arrange their leaves so that each one receives maximum exposure to light – hence the delightful, single thickness of overlapping ivy (*Hedera* species and varieties) or Boston ivy (*Parthenocissus tricuspidata*) leaves that clothe external walls like textured wallpaper. Indoors, self-clingers such as ivy need moisture for their aerial roots to cling to a support such as a moss pole or internal brick wall; regularly mist spraying, if practical, helps. Meandering branches of ivy (*Hedera* species and varieties) or creeping fig (*Ficus pumila*), a diminutive-leaved self clinger, could then wander, divide and subdivide along a brick living-room wall like the tributaries of a river, forming an abstract pattern perhaps punctuated by an 'island' painting, print or poster.

Climbing or trailing houseplants without aerial roots can be encouraged to create a similar effect, by tying their evenly spaced-out lax stems to a large, wall-fixed framework of closely spaced wires, poles or slats. (Black- or red-painted metal grids, or even shiny metal ones, can add their own contribution to the decor, fixed to a white wall.) The cup-and-saucer vine (*Cobaea scandens*) and the Chilean glory vine (*Eccremocarpus scaber*) cling by means of tendrils and, once given initial support, rapidly get on with it. Even non-self-supporting trailers such as ivy-leaved pelargoniums (*Pelargonium peltatum* varieties and hybrids) can create a wallpaper-like expanse of foliage and flowers, given enough light, food, water and gentle direction.

A high-level, narrow wall shelf offers the potential for a broad expanse of trailing foliage and flowers, whether from a single substantial plant – a grape ivy (*Rhoicissus rhomboidea*) or Swedish ivy (*Plectranthus* species), for example

Hang ups

△ These epiphytic grey *tillandsias*, or air plants, have furry leaf scales that absorb minute nutrients and water from the atmosphere. They are glued or wired to cork, rocks, shells, driftwood or pieces of coral.

In the round

▷ Wall-fixed, circular metal ring brackets hold a mixed selection of foliage houseplants. Ring brackets are good indoors or out, ideally against a waterproof wall surface. In internal timber stud walls, you need to locate the studs first, and screw the brackets to them.

– or a mixed group. Or group several plants tightly or loosely – all of one type, two different varieties in repeated or chequerboard fashion or a mixed medley – in several rows, one plant thick, against a wall. Those with naturally arching or trailing growth habits can help counteract the formal divisions of shelves or brackets and mingle with neighbours; those with long, threadlike stems and occasional leaves or plantlets – hearts entwined (*Ceropegia*

woodii), spider plant (*Chlorophytum comosum* 'Vittatum') or mother-of-thousands (*Saxifraga sarmentosa*) for example – can connect several rows in a delicate, filmy curtain. And sculptural, flat-stemmed plants such as opuntia cacti (*Opuntia* species) can act as focal points, especially if repeated here and there.

Firmly three-dimensional houseplants – rosette-forming types, for example, or tree-like types – grown as wallpaper against a solid wall, with light coming from a directional source, benefit from being given a quarter turn every week or two, if practical. This prevents leaves and branches in permanent shade from becoming pale and drawn and, ultimately, dying. And as with trellis work or other forms of plant support in the garden, try to leave at least a 2.5 cm(1 in) gap between the support and the wall, in order to allow air to circulate and room for twiners to twine.

Room Dividers

Houseplants can be used to separate one functional area from another – the dining and living areas of an open-plan layout, for example, or the desk/workspace and recreational area in a living room. Unlike solid walls, houseplants create a sense of enclosure while still allowing through sound and a glimpse of activity beyond. And depending on the type and juxtaposition of plants, light can also penetrate from one area to another – important in small open-plan houses in which solid walls might be claustrophobic and dark. When children share a bedroom, a barrier of houseplants (heavy enough not to be knocked over or otherwise out of reach!) can give each child a sense of privacy and territory while maintaining the spatial integrity of the room.

Any plant 'qualifies' for the job. Large, floor-level plants can be lined up like a row of soldiers to divide the areas in question, or embrace one area like an armchair. Medium-sized plants can be displayed on cupboards and shelves of various heights, used to divide the spaces. Glass shelves allow maximum light to reach the plants and create a pretty, floating effect, with plants seemingly hovering in space. Make sure the glass is strong enough: plate or float glass, the thickness depending on span but a minimum of 15 mm (½ in). Toughened glass is stronger but more expensive. Consult your glazier or supplier, giving the span and approximate load.

Built-in plant troughs, once fashionable, can be attractive room dividers but are inflexible in terms of layout and demand ongoing commitment. Movable plant troughs are better – garden centres are the best source.

Trailing plants can hang from floor-standing shelves or shelves or baskets suspended from the ceiling joists. Small plants can form a vertical patchwork on narrowly spaced shelves, perhaps interspersed with decorative objects. For a light-hearted solution, train climbing plants such as ivy (*Hedera* species and cultivars), kangaroo vine (*Cissus antarctica*) or grape ivy (*Rhoicissus rhomboidea*) up and over old-fashioned brass post-and-rope cordons, or through white-painted picket fences, perhaps around a dining table and chairs; a grass-green carpet and sky-blue ceiling would complete the *trompe l'oeil*.

Trellis, another garden feature, can be used indoors as a room divider and plant support. Brace flat trellis panels and bolt to the floor or fix with batten 'feet'. Free-standing, ivy-covered trellis pyramids can mark the imaginary corners of a dining area, with low shelves or cupboards between; three trellis panels can be connected and angled to form a climber-covered screen, gently reflecting the curves of a table, or concealing a sink in a bedroom.

Living partition

◁ A boisterous vine, intertwined with a Madagascar dragon tree, divides the 'music room' from the living room proper, while still allowing complete circulation and daylight through. Its looping stems create a lively and slowly changing bas–relief against the white wall.

Screen star

△ A tubular-metal stair railing provides support for variegated ivy on a landing, with room for expansion at a later date along the railings to the lower floor. The leaves arrange themselves naturally into a screen one leaf thick, giving maximum cover.

Indoor jungle

Mixed and modest foliage plants, including palm, Madagascar dragon tree, sweetheart plant, and various ferns and begonias, are unmemorable individually, but unite to create a pleasing, indoor jungle. The windowsills, shelves and stools on which the plants are placed are used as substitute stems, to vary the plants' heights – a very easy but effective display idea.

Communal Members

Many houseplants are modest – naturally small or smaller versions of large, specimen plants; perhaps with no, few or small flowers and unmemorable leaves. None the less, such plants are popular because they are cheap, almost universally available and make instant gifts or comforting impulse purchases. Not every houseplant can be a 'star' and like ordinary-looking, unexceptional children that happen to be yours, you love them anyway and want to display them with pride.

Grouping such houseplants is an effective way to do this; it may be worth buying three or four more to augment those you already have. Consider the space between the plant group in the same way that you would consider the 'negative' space between objects in a still life drawing or painting. Though there are exceptions, evenly spaced-out plants often convey a sense of formality and isolation rather than community. Small-leaved spreaders – ivies (*Hedera* species and varieties), creeping fig (*Ficus pumila*), wandering Jews (*Tradescantia* species and varieties, *Zebrina* species) or Swedish ivy (*Plectranthus* species), for example – are invaluable in communal displays. Though they have no architectural form of their own, they act as a unifying element, whether filling the horizontal space between pots or forming a vertical shower of greenery.

Don't be afraid to rest small pots on the potting compost of larger pots, Tower-of-Babel fashion. Each raised pot helps break the boring rhythm of rows of single-level pots and if trailing plants are rested on other pots, the foliage helps further 'obfuscate' the regularity. On a practical level, watering is easier and the microclimate is beneficial to those houseplants liking a bit of humidity. Move the

Four of a kind

Mind-your-own-business, or baby's tears (*Soleirolia soleirolii*) comes in plain green, the all-gold 'Aurea' or 'Golden Green', and 'Argentea', 'Silver Queen' or 'Variegata', the green-and-white variegated forms. Its mossy growth has long been valued as ground-covering carpet under greenhouse staging but as individual globes of foliage they can be mixed and matched, as instant topiary.

smaller pot around the potting compost in the larger pot from time to time, to allow air to reach the host plant's roots.

Alternately, add height and rhythm by raising occasional plants on upturned flower pots. Ideally, use identical terracotta pots; the narrow-necked angle that the pots create is pleasantly sculptural and if you can get old, hand-thrown pots, the minor irregularities and rough surface add to the effect.

A tight group of massed, communal plants can create a focal point in the same way that a single, large specimen plant can. Fill a corner with communal plants; the right-angled walls act as a natural frame. The communal approach can include large plants as well; a single, large, tree-like plant can act as the keystone for a cluster of medium-sized and smaller plants, like the natural community of woodland trees, shrubs, climbers and wild flowers.

Collector's Items

Interest may focus on a particular type of houseplant, whether a single genus, such as *Saintpaulia*, the African violet, or a group such as desert cacti, comprised of many genera. The attraction may be their beauty – orchids, for example; sculptural character, as with cacti or air plants; or even curiosity mixed with mild revulsion, as with carnivorous plants. The objective, occasionally bordering on obsession, may be one of crude numbers, amassing as many as possible; of rarity value, growing the most unusual or challenging forms; or of archetypal perfection – nurturing half a dozen plants embodying the Platonic ideal of the type. Once 'hooked', a whole new world beckons: specialist nurseries, books and horticultural societies, with their meetings, shows, competitions and mutual support.

Collections, by their nature, imply long-term commitment, so before embarking, make sure you can meet the basic heat, light, space and care requirements of the type of plant being considered. Carnivorous plants, for example, are very demanding and diffi-cult; traditional bonsai plants require outdoor conditions. Artificial lighting can be used to augment or as a substitute for natural daylight – in a cellar perhaps, or dark corner; use 'nat-ural white' fluorescent tubes, on their own or combined with 'daylight' fluorescent tubes. African violets respond especially well to arti-ficial light.

Display possibilities range from the coldly botanical exhibition, with subjects equally spaced, labelled and ordered, to the re-creation in miniature of the landscape in which the plants would be found naturally. The collection can be in uniform, neutral containers, focusing interest on the plants or

in varied decorative containers, attractive in their own right. Plant-filled tables, shelves, trolleys and racks such as bakers' racks can form part of the decor of a room, perhaps act-ing as room dividers, as well as housing the display. Some collector's plants suggest their own stage setting: an epiphytic tree for bromeliads, for example, or glass fish tank for humidity-loving members of the *Gesneriaceae* family: episcias (*Episcia* species) and miniature gloxinias (*Sinningia speciosa* hybrids).

Move plants in flower or at the height of beauty to a prominent position such as a dining-room table and back to a less promi-

nent position afterwards to rest; rotating plants allows them to be fully enjoyed and keeps you in touch with the natural growth cycle.

The importance of adding only healthy, pest- and disease-free new plants to a collection cannot be overstressed. It is even worth keeping new introductions in isolation for a couple of weeks, because monocultures, whether thousands of acres of a single variety of wheat or a room filled with dozens of African violets, are especially vulnerable to infection or infestation. Try, too, to keep the the paraphernalia of propagation and ailing plants well away from prime display areas.

Sunny side up

This intense yellow background, foreground and flowerpots could be toned down and adapted for 'normal' living quarters. Mixed orchids make up most of this collection, with a few spring-flowering bulbs: grape hyacinths, hippeastrum and narcissi, so the real unifying theme is verticality!

EASY COLLECTOR'S PLANTS

African violets
  (*Saintpaulia ionan-tha* hybrids)
Bromeliads
  Aechmea
  Ananas
  Billbergia
  Cryptanthus
  Guzmania
  Neoregelia
  Tillandsia
  Vriesia
Cacti
  Cephalocereus
  Cereus
  Chamaecereus
  Echinocactus
  Ferocactus
  Gymnocalycium
  Mammilaria
  Notocactus
  Opuntia
  Rebutia
  Trichocereus
Orchids
  Cattleya
  Cymbidium
  Cypripedium
  Coelygone
  Miltonia
  Odontoglossum
Pelargoniums
  (*Pelargonium* species
  and hybrids)
Succulents
  Aeonium
  Aloe
  Bryophyllum
  Crassula
  Gasteria
  Haworthia
  Kalanchoe
  Sedum

Prickly business

Cacti – often short, fat and prickly – may be considered the ugly ducklings of the plant world but their strong sculptural characters, wide availability, low cost if bought young, easy cultivation, slow growth and brilliant flowers, often from a surprisingly young age, make them favourite subjects for collecting.

Cacti collections often contain succulents as well; technically, the presence of aereoles, cushion-like, modified sideshoots carrying spines and/or hairs, is what distinguishes cacti from their look-alike relatives. Flowers and offsets grow from aereoles and each aereole flowers only once.

This collection features barrel- and ball-shaped cacti: *Opuntias* including the yellow-tufted *O. microdasys*, or bunny ears; the man-made 'Hibotan', or red-capped cacti, consisting of the red *Gymnocalycium mihanovichii* grafted on to a green cactus base; plus two succulents: the moonstone or sugared almond plant, *Pachyphytum oviferum*, and partridge-breast aloe, *Aloe variegata*.

Containers

Flowerpots

CONTAINERS ARE AN integral part of any houseplant display with as much creative potential as the choice of plants. A nasty container can detract from a magnificent houseplant and a 'nothing' houseplant can become a 'star' in a super container, while neutral, terracotta pots fill the vast realm of the acceptable in between.

Flowerpots are the obvious, functional containers and traditional terracotta goes well with almost any decor except the ornate or purely formal. Many people find that terracotta, as a natural material, looks better with plants than plastic pots. But snobbery about all things plastic is perhaps unwise, since there are horticultural advantages to plastic, including weight, cost and ease of watering, cleaning, sterilizing and storing. Do note, however, that black plastic pots, like black carpets, show up dirt surprisingly well, and except for purposely kitsch decor, plastic flowerpots mimicking woven basketwork or classical china are bound to disappoint, because the rim's thinness reveals all.

Traditional, hand-thrown terracotta flowerpots, with their rough surface and asymmetry, can be difficult to find. Most garden centres carry smooth, symmetrical manufactured ones, often in a slightly harsh orange tone. Placed in the garden, however, they eventually mellow or you can use one of the instant mellowing techniques given below. Garden centres also stock terracotta pots and rectangular planters and troughs with bas-relief decorations and glazed terracotta pots. Oriental glazed earthenware pots can be especially pleasing, with subtle or deep, intense colours and delicate, textural effects.

Terracotta flowerpots can be stencilled (as shown here), opaquely painted or lightly colour-washed with acrylic paints, full strength or diluted; colour-washes are ideal to pick out bas-relief. Terracotta can also be tinted with children's chalks and then coated with polyurethane varnish. Colour-washing or chalking can add an instant patina to a new pot, especially if dull greens, greys, browns, ochres or white are used; alternatively, colour-washing and tinting can pick up the colours of a decor — say, royal blue or crimson — and create a colour co-ordinated, 'designer' look.

Stencil brushes
Marine sponge
Paper towel
Tape measure
Flexible, ready-made stencil, or home-made stencil
  cut with a craft knife from thin card or acetate
Paper and pencil
Masking tape
Cocktail stick

1 Paint the base colour, including well inside the rim, and paint the insides with polyurethane varnish, to prevent moisture lifting the paintwork. Allow to dry. For a sponged effect, pour a little paint into a saucer and stir smooth with a cocktail stick. Dip in a natural, marine sponge, dab off excess paint on to a paper towel until you are happy with the coverage, then apply. Each time you re-wet the sponge, remember to dab off excess. Allow to dry.

2 Roughly work out how you want the design to look. For a repeating pattern that requires moving the stencil, work out the spacing, using a tape measure and pencil.

3 Have a trial run first. Tape the stencil on to a piece of paper, pour paint into a saucer, stir until smooth with a cocktail stick and dip the brush in. Dab off excess paint on to a paper towel, then using the brush vertically, dab paint on to each cut-out shape, working from the edge to the middle. Every time you re-wet the brush, remove excess paint.

4 Once you master the technique, tape the stencil flat against the flowerpot surface and paint in all the cut-out shapes.

5 Carefully remove, clean and dry the stencil. Once the paintwork is dry, reposition the stencil and repeat the pattern, if necessary.

6 Before painting a second colour, clean all stencils, equipment and brushes thoroughly with soap and water. Proceed as before, lining up the stencil with the motifs already painted.

Patterned pots

This collection of stencilled flowerpots in variations of blue and white has a charming, rural appeal, and once you set things up, it's almost as easy to make several as one. Simple motifs are easiest to execute and 'read' but you can mix and match them to your heart's content. Using sample pots of paint where possible keeps costs down. A white base coat is shown but you can stencil directly on to terracotta.

New, smooth, terracotta flowerpots
Masonry paints
Polyurethane varnish

Cachepots

Cachepots, literally meaning 'hide pots', are decorative outer containers that conceal an inner pot, and can be made of almost any material. The flowerpot should always sit well in it, with its rim below the rim of the *cachepot* and, ideally, top dressing (see page 67) taking up any slack between the two. A *cachepot* that is too deep can be filled inside with crumpled, wire-mesh netting, wooden blocks or marbles to bring the levels up.

Like terracotta, baskets made from natural materials associate well with houseplants. Whether willow, the most common raw material, or rowan, hazel, oak, reed, rush, grass, bamboo, palm, lavender, vine or moss, their irregularity and hand-made quality give them a homely charm. Natural colours range from palest straw to green, rich honey or deep brown, depending on the raw material and its treatment.

Some baskets are woven of dyed components or dyed or painted as finished articles. One or more colours can be used, in more or less natural tones and a variety of patterns or textures, African, Oriental and South American basketry being particularly lovely. You can paint or dye your own natural, un-varnished baskets, to match the plants or decor or ideally both. For a rich, intense matt colour, use two coats of emulsion paint. Aerosol spray paints can look dense or airy, according to distance from the object sprayed and number of coats. For subtle, transparent stains, use undiluted artists' inks, rubbed on with a soft cloth, then coated with polyurethane varnish. As well as single colours, you can use two near-miss colours such as pink and apricot; strongly contrasting ones such as red and blue; or multicolours, bearing in mind the colour created by any overlap.

Baskets which originally had another func-

Brilliant blue

The grape hyacinths and inexpensive, round wicker basket, painted deep royal blue to match, have a doubly powerful impact.

The basket is painted with full-strength matt emulsion. For a more translucent colour wash you can water down the paint, but try various strengths first on paper, to get the effect you want, before painting the basket.

tion can be used: laundry, log, garden or shopping baskets; waste-paper baskets; French loaf baskets; slatted wooden orchid baskets or even little sewing baskets. With their simple, functional form, they are often more appealing than coy or over-decorated baskets produced for the floristry and houseplant trade. Baskets woven in the shape of animals – frogs, mallard ducks or elephants, for example – can be charming, sprouting their own greenery camouflage.

To extend the life of a basket, line it with polythene before placing the flowerpots in

Midwinter magic

Winter-flowering iris (*I. reticulata*) are much smaller and more modest than the showy German, or flag, iris, that typify summer borders, but are valued for their early colour. Here, they make a temporary indoor display, their pots concealed by a raffia-tied bundle of winter stems.

Plant the bulbs in autumn and fix the twiggy covering through which the leaves and flowers emerge, as described below, or buy pots of bulbs in flower and work the covering round and through them. In this case, follow steps 2 and 3, but insert the twigs gently and carefully between the actual plants.

Iris reticulata bulbs
Crocks or gravel
Loam or peat-based potting compost
2 flowerpots
Dried stems or branches such as grapevine,
   knotweed, cow parsley, dogwood or birch, 4
   times as long as the pot diameter

1 Place a layer of drainage material in the base of the flowerpots. Part-fill with potting compost, then plant 6–8 bulbs, and cover with 2.5cm (1in) of potting compost, to come 15–25mm (½–1in) below the rim. Water lightly.

2 Lay two parallel, 45cm (18in) long raffia pieces on a work surface, slightly less than the stems' or branches' width apart. Place a layer of stems or branches on top and at right angles to the raffia. Place the two pots, side by side, in the middle. Make two parallel, generous piles of branches or stems, one in front and one at the back of the pots, again at right angles to the raffia.

3 Lift the ends of the raffia, easing the branches or stems up and over the pots, adding more if necessary to conceal completely the pots. (It is easier if you have someone to help you). Leaving spaces for the leaves and flowers to push through, tightly tie the raffia.

4 Place outdoors in a sheltered, sunny spot. Water only when growth shows and, once flower buds are showing colour, bring indoors.

Crafty

△ Hand-painted barge-
ware and American
tollware often have
patterns based on simpli-
fied floral themes. Here,
stylized pink roses inspire
the choice of cut flower –
matching, hot-pink

White on white

▷ A cluster of disparate
containers becomes
visually unified if they all
share a common colour
theme – in this case white,
although technically, white
is the absence of colour.
Sharing a common
material, glazed china,
also helps.

it, or place the pots on a saucer or flexible, aluminium-foil freezer bowl or tray, which can be slightly crushed to fit.

Informal wooden *cachepots* include garden trugs and sieves; salad bowls; and for larger plants or plant grouping, beer barrel halves. More formal are white, green or black-painted wooden Versailles tubs, for large specimen plants; and decorative wooden boxes, their lids propped open, for small displays.

Ceramic and china *cachepots* are probably the most popular. Many are sold as just that, glazed or unglazed, decorated or plain, in a range of shapes and sizes, including woven basketry; stylized shells; stylized swans, pigs, rhinoceri and leopards; classical caryatids or cherubs sup-

porting china bowls; and hollow busts, with flowers and foliage providing the 'hair'. Traditional jardinières with matching stands are the ultimate *cachepot*.

Glass receptacles are virtually always water-tight, and as primary containers, are most suitable for terrariums (see pages 50–51), forced hyacinth and daffodils bulbs and tender waterside plants, such as the umbrella plant, *Cyperus alternifolius*, or variegated sweet flag, *Acorus gramineus* 'Variegatus'. With careful watering, however, almost any plant can be grown in a flowerpot placed inside a much larger glass container, such as a battery jar, with the striations of drainage material, such as gravel, shells, wood bark, moss, dried funghi and potting compost, becoming a feature. As smaller *cachepots*, it is better to use only opaque or translucent glass such as blue Bristol, cranberry or ruby glass.

Metal *cachepots* range from traditional pewter, brass, iron or copper mugs, jugs, coal scuttles, preserving pans; old-fashioned, per-forated room heaters and wine coolers to printed tin boxes and enamelled, cast-iron French kitchenware, perhaps with a burnt or chipped bottom, but too beautiful and expen-sive to throw away. Lead planters and troughs, and fibreglass lookalikes, are usually used out-doors but could equally well be used inside. American Colonial-style toleware dustbins, letter boxes, pitchers or watering cans with print or hand-painted decorations, would make attractive *cachepots*. At the bottom end of the market, there are empty paint or food tins, brightly painted or decorated with paper collages and 'antiqued' with varnish.

Last, plastic should not be dismissed alto-gether: simple modern plastic planters have merit, and 'fun' type plastic storage boxes can be *cachepots* – it is only when plastic mas-querades as what it's not, that it look wrong. Plastic baskets, for example, range from dubious willow look-alikes to strong, excit-ing, contemporary design statements.

Terrariums

Terrariums are self-contained worlds in miniature. Part of their fascination lies in our temporarily divine-like ability to create them, and part in their capacity to be self-maintaining.

Use clear or lightly tinted green glass containers which can be completely or largely closed. Fishbowls, aquariums and green glass carboys are traditional, as are Victorian-style lead-and-glass Ward cases. Less conventional choices include geometric glass vases, cider jugs, pitchers, battery jars, wide-mouthed preserving jars, confectionery jars, glass mixing bowls and casseroles, and even narrow, spaghetti storage jars. For children, glass baby-food jars can each hold one or two tiny plants, to make a collection of miniature terrariums. Flat-sided jars can be planted and displayed on their sides, as well as upright. Avoid plastic containers, which suffer from build-up of condensation on the sides, and can become scratched, brittle and discoloured.

Choose warmth- and humidity-loving, naturally dwarf or slow-growing plants, and take as much care in juxtaposing contrasting form, colour and texture as you would in designing a full-sized garden. The landscape can be formal or informal: twee, with tiny china bridges, mirrored pools and paths of birdcage gravel; or unadorned, relying solely on plants, pebbles and stones for landscape imagery.

Decide whether the display is front facing, or to be seen from all sides. For a conventional landscape, place a layer of drainage material in the bottom, mounding it if wished, then a 5–10 cm (2–4 in) layer of peat-based potting compost. (For maneuvering in narrow-necked containers, tape a fork and a teaspoon on to long bamboo canes.) Ideally, try out plants in various positions before planting. Plant firmly, water lightly, and leave in a shady spot for a few days. Most terrarium plants need bright light but never leave terrariums in direct sunlight.

PLANTS FOR TERRARIUMS

Aluminium plant (*Pilea cadierei*)
Bird's-nest fern (*Asplenium nidus-avis*)
Brake ferns (*Pteris cretica*)
Button fern (*Pellaea rotundifolia*)
Calathea (*Calathea* species)
Creeping fig (*Ficus pumila*)
Earth stars (*Cryptanthus* species)
Fittonia (*Fittonia* species)
Ivy (*Hedera helix* varieties)
Maidenhair fern (*Adiantum capillus-veneris*)
Moss ferns (*Selaginella* species)
Mother-of-thousands (*Saxifraga stolonifera* 'Tricolor')
Polypody fern (*Polypodium vulgare*)
Prayer plant (*Maranta leuconeura kerchoveana*)
Tradescantia (*Tradescantia* species)
Variegated sweetflag (*Acorus gramineus* 'Variegatus')

Mossy duo

Largely or entirely enclosed terrariums are self-maintaining because moisture released by plants during transpiration condenses on the container's sides or top and returns to the potting compost, to be taken up again by the plants. Unlike the narrow-necked vase shown, the glass tumbler's open top precludes long-term self-maintenance, though the display, kept cool, damp and bright, should last for a couple of weeks. Alternatively, make the moss, lichen, liverwort, bark and stone column shorter and cover with a glass disc, or use dried moss and plant material.

Glass vase
Glass tumbler
Peat-based potting compost
Bun moss
Sphagnum moss
Lichen-covered stones and/or bark
Liverwort-covered stones and/or bark
Long tweezers or fork taped to a bamboo rod

1 Pour a layer of peat-based potting compost in the bottom of the vase.

2 Using the tweezers or fork, cover the potting compost with a layer of mixed moss, then build up a central mound of moss. Spray lightly.

3 Build up a 'living' column of moss, stones and/or bark in the tumbler, using the tweezers or fork to ensure that the moss clumps face outwards and tapping the tumbler gently, to settle the contents. Spray lightly.

4 Clean the inside of the glass if necessary, using damp cotton wool.

Moss, bark and leaves

Moss, cork and bark are plants or parts of plants, and containers made from those materials can resemble extensions of the houseplant itself, or create a naturalistic knoll-like setting.

Imported, fresh moss baskets are charming and relatively inexpensive; unfortunately, their clear green colour eventually fades to beige. Bun moss turns a pleasing silvery green as it dries, and reindeer moss, a silvery white. You can glue dried moss, in single or mixed types, to plastic pots, shallow wooden crates or tin cans to create 'up-market' outer containers, unique and costly-looking in their slight unevenness. Try to continue the mossy theme by using moss as a mulch, or top dressing, on the potting compost, even if temporarily.

Cork oak bark (*Quercus suber*) can also be used as an outer finish to otherwise dull containers; a slightly uneven top edge adds to the rustic quality. Cork oak is often used to line the back and sides of aquariums, and is available at specialist tropical fish shops. Trees that produce usably large sections of peeling bark, for glueing in overlapping layers to a container, include plane (*Platanus* species) and eucalyptus, but these you will have to collect yourself. At a pinch, coat the sides of an inexpensive container with glue, then roll or press it into a spread-out layer of pulverized, sterilized bark, of the kind normally used for mulching flowerbeds and borders and available in bags from garden centres.

Bas relief

Twigs, including red-barked dogwood, lichens, mosses and various leaves, transform a plastic flower-pot into a low bas relief, as handsome and exotic as the anthurium it contains.

Use the basic technique given in the recipe opposite, but base juxta-positions on contrast in colour, form and texture and aim for an abstract, random effect.

Anthuriums can be tricky, needing continually warm, humid, draught-free conditions, bright but indirect light and frequent but restrained watering with soft, tepid water.

Black magic

This exquisite *cachepot* is made from Italian, dyed, preserved magnolia leaves. Order them through your florist or use glycerined magnolia (*Magnolia grandiflora*), beech (*Fagus sylvatica*), laurel (*Prunus laurocerasus*) or Portugal laurel (*Prunus lusitanica*) leaves, in shades of rich brown, instead. Three rows of leaves are shown; adjust numbers for larger or smaller pots, or larger or smaller leaves, accordingly. A professional, florist's hot-glue gun was used but a strong, household glue will do. (Avoid fiercely strong glues, however, since you are likely to get some glue on your fingers.)

Plastic flowerpot
Hot-glue gun or strong household glue
Flexible, preserved leaves
Twine
Polyurethane varnish

1 Starting on the top row, glue a leaf to the pot so that it protrudes slightly above the rim. Working in one direction, glue the next leaf so it overlaps the first as far as the central midrib, and press firmly. Continue glueing until the top row is finished.
2 Repeat the procedure with a middle row of leaves, making sure there are no gaps between the two rows. Continue with a third row, bending the leaves under as necessary.
3 Tie with garden twine, then spray with polyurethane varnish, to protect the leaves and give them a slight sheen. Allow to dry before using.

ALTERNATIVES
You can cut out leaves from illustrated magazines or boldy printed floral fabrics, glue them on the flower pot in overlapping layers and varnish or spray them, découpage fashion, or iron leaves – leaves with autumn tints are ideal – between sheets of waxed paper and proceed as before. End the leaves at the rim, since none of these materials is tough or stiff enough to stand up above it.

Unusual Options

Anything hollow and stable is a potential container or *cachepot*. Terracotta chimney pots, stone urns or bonsai pots (which can be used for cacti, succulents and dwarf bulbs) from the garden; wooden or old-fashioned wirework bird cages; giant clam shells and conch shells; flexible straw shopping baskets; woven hemp or coir African handbags; trophies; cat or dog feeding bowls – the options are as wide as the imagination.

Old-fashioned Edwardian prams, or baby carriages, built to last for ever, can hold large plants or plant groups, as can bassinets, wooden or wicker cradles, and cots or cribs; plant-filled, doll-sized versions of the above, especially if old and made of natural materials, would look lovely in an older child's bedroom. A plant-filled, wickerwork shopping basket in the hall combines the transitional, 'just about to go' quality of the setting with the permanence of plants in a gentle pun. (In the summer, you could wheel the plant out to the garden; likewise, plant-filled prams or plant-filled, old-fashioned, children's toy wooden wagons.)

If you water carefully, old-fashioned wooden hat boxes, papier mâché storage boxes or modern, papercovered cardboard gift boxes could be used, or you could make your own, perhaps using left-over wallpaper or giftwrap paper reproducing classic designs such as eighteenth-century English floral, Art Deco or Art Nouveau patterns.

For instant improvising, look at kitchen ceramic and china containers: huge, rabbit- or cauliflower-shaped soup tureens; pint and half-pint coffee mugs; empty soft drink tins; stoneware preserve jars; kettles, teapots and coffeepots; gravy boats; large and small soufflé

Sandy business

△ Though this display looks like a freshly cut section of opuntia propped in a jar of coloured sand purely as an 'art shot', artistic licence can be the source of real design possibilities. You could pour layers of coloured sand into the space between a flowerpot and outer glass container or, more simply, use alternating colours of chippings or tropical fish gravel.

Naming names

▷ A corral of children's toy blackboards hides the flower pots in an indoor herb garden and names the tarragon, mint, lavender, rosemary and thyme within, albeit in French.

A pretty biscuit tin could do a similar job, visually and physically containing a cluster of small plants that might otherwise come to grief in a busy kitchen.

dishes; bread bins, and storage tins. Wirework lettuce shakers can be lined with moss, filled with a hanging houseplant and used as a hanging basket. Even wooden eggcups can hold tiny cacti; and French wirework eggstands, tiny epiphytes, each wirework cup first lined in moss.

Props

Shells, Wood and Stones

HOUSEPLANTS, HOWEVER GENETICALLY tampered with, symbolize the natural world; any attractive natural object, organic or inorganic, that also appears as an extension of nature is a potential prop. Placed next to a houseplant, the object creates a visual partnership and anchor and if it conceals part or all of a plastic flowerpot, so much the better. Large, natural props can be used singly, as statues, smaller ones can be grouped to form multiple displays or suggest the beginnings of a landscape or seascape – just experiment, readjusting, mixing and matching until you are pleased with the results.

Tropical fish shops specializing in marine fish sell shells, as do some museums, specialist craft shops and seaside souvenir shops – ironically, the shells are often imported from thousands of miles away. (If collecting shells from a beach, make sure first that they are not protected by conservation laws.) Ordinary scallop shells can be tucked vertically into the back of a small, plant-filled flowerpot, as an Art-Deco-style sunburst backdrop, or a row of scallop shells displayed vertically behind and slightly above a row of small houseplants.

A shallow glass bowl of tiny turk's cap shells in mixed colours can repeat the main colours of variegated foliage. The sensual, flesh pink inner surface of a conch shell can reinforce the pink of miniature roses or of orchids; the mother-of-pearl of an ormer or abalone shell can reflect an adjacent white-flowered plant.

Larger shells can contain plants. A tropical fluted clam shell can be a young child's delight, planted with tiny cacti or succulent offsets, or moss and rooted ivy sprigs; or, for a more sophisticated effect, planted with a single mound of mind-your-own-business (*Soleirolia soleirolii*). Air plants (grey *Tillandsia* species), that derive both nutrients and water from the air, are often sold glued to monovalve shells or coral, the skeletal remains of millions of tiny sea creatures.

Sun-bleached driftwood or dead tree ivy roots, with their twisted, sculptural form, make good neighbours for houseplants, the juxtaposition of living and dead again repeat-

Crystal colour

The clear, pure purple of *Streptocarpus*, or Cape primrose, flowers are repeated in the crystals of an amethyst geode, which would look equally attractive with African violets or the velvety purple leaves of *Gynura aurantica*.

Geodes are hollow rocks containing small cavities lined with crystals or other mineral matter; half geodes often have the rich, lush quality of a halved pomegranate. You can buy geodes in their country of origin – South America, Africa and Asia for amethysts – or, more conveniently but more expensively, from science and geology museums, or specialist shops.

Streptocarpus are tropical plants, needing medium to bright light, high humidity in hot weather, generous watering from spring to autumn, and minimal watering in winter.

ing nature. A rectangular section of tree ivy root can be inserted into potting compost at the back of a flowerpot, like an extraordinarily ornate Spanish comb, for climbing plants to wander up or simply to extend interest vertically. (Flat, fan coral can be used in a similar way.) Or the tree ivy root can be rested in front of a flowerpot, to counteract its visual solidity.

Smooth, fluid-shaped pebbles and larger stones are available for free from shingle beaches or swift-flowing streams. You can buy sections of geodes, with their secret, crystal-lined hollow centres, from geology museums, for displaying next to houseplants. Polished cross-sections of rose quartz, agate and other semi-precious minerals can make a theatrical, halo-like background frame, displayed vertically behind a small houseplant. Pebbles and chippings can form decorative mulches piled up in a glass bowl or battery tank to conceal flowerpots (see page 48).

Large chunks of striated sandstone, large flints with their black and white contrast – any attractive stone is a potential abstract sculpture, and like 'proper' sculpture, the stone and its accompanying houseplant should be displayed in a carefully planned setting, whether based on the airiness of a modern museum or the controlled clutter of a Victorian sitting room.

Fruit and Vegetables

These are part of the same, organic visual language as houseplants and make natural display partners for them. Fresh fruit and vegetables can be temporary 'houseplant' displays in their own right – a trug or wicker basket planted with strawberry plants in fruit, complete with graceful runners, for example, or an ornamental lettuce such as 'Red Salad Bowl', carefully dug up with a good-sized rootball and planted in damp potting compost in a terracotta pot. If they are kept cool and mist-sprayed regularly, they will last for two days or more before needing replanting outdoors, discarding or eating – certainly long enough to grace a summer luncheon or dinner party table.

Fruits and vegetables can act as a decorative mulch (see page 67) and also as containers. Any large, flat-based or stable fruit or vegetable that can be stuffed – pineapples, aubergines, marrows, beefsteak tomatoes and melons, for example – can be scooped out and filled with one, or more houseplants for a temporary display.

Fruits and vegetables can emphasize floral or foliage colour: a big bowl of lemons, for example, next to a pot of forced daffodils or yellow chrysanthemums; red, or Bermuda, onions or plums picking up the rich tones of wine-red polyanthus; or even pink and white spring turnips displayed near a similarly coloured coleus.

As well as fresh fruits and vegetables, you can prop houseplants with dried gourds or Indian corn, or facsimile fruit and vegetables in wood, china, pottery, semi-precious minerals, wicker, glass, metal, papier mâché, fabric or even kitsch plastic. Ethnic and craft shops are rich hunting grounds for make-

believe fruit and vegetables, both mundane and exotic, and unlike the 'real thing' artificial fruits and vegetables can form a lifelong collection. Remember that fresh fruit and vegetables emit ethylene gas, which hastens plant development and shortens the display life of certain flowers such as orchids, especially in warm conditions.

Berried treasure

Winter cherries are cheap and showy but their growth habit can be ungainly, so massing them creates the best display. Azaleas, another winter favourite, can also have an awkward growth habit and, though costlier, can be used in the same way.

3 winter cherry houseplants
Fresh sphagnum moss
Peat-based potting compost
Small ornamental gourds
Pine cones
Deep ceramic or china bowl

1 Place the plants, in their pots or out, in the centre of a deep bowl, so the surface of the rootballs comes 2.5cm (1in) or more below the bowl rim. If the rootball is too high, gently tease out a little potting compost from the base of the rootball.
2 Pack the spaces between the pots or rootballs with damp, peat-based potting compost, tapping the bowl as you proceed, to settle the potting compost.
3 Place a layer of fresh sphagnum moss over the rootballs and potting compost, tucking it well under the plants.
4 Stud the moss with a scattering of dried gourds and pine cones, sprayed first with polyurethane varnish, if wished, for an attractive, subtle sheen. (At Christmas, rest tiny silver Christmas-tree balls on the moss, and hang a few on the plants.)

Triples

Small pots of winter cherries on a mantelpiece reinforce the main ingredient of the focal point display (*see right*).

The wand-like cut sprays of ornamental pepper continue the orange theme, and could also be used with Christmas peppers.

Both winter cherries and Christmas peppers need cool, bright conditions, moist potting compost and high humidity.

Paintings and Murals

Houseplants are never seen in isolation, like a subject on a microscopic slide, but as part of the immediate and then larger, setting. By using images of plants as the immediate setting, you can confuse the division between the two- and the three-dimensional, each adding intrigue to the other.

A painting or poster with a floral or foliar theme can add coherence to a disparate plant group, or add gravitas to a single plant. The images can be realistic or interpretive, ranging from delicate, nineteenth-century botanical prints to the huge, almost overwhelmingly larger-than-life, flowers of the American artist Georgia O'Keeffe; the much-loved water lilies of Monet; the painstakingly detailed verdure of the Pre-Raphaelites such as Dante Gabriel Rossetti and Holman Hunt; or the flat, child-like work of primitives such as Henri Rousseau.

Photographic posters of Dutch bulb fields in flower, tropical rainforests – use anything predominantly leafy or flowery that you like, can live with and fits comfortably in the room. On a tight budget, top-quality gift-wrapping paper based on flowers and foliage can merit framing. Changing the images seasonally or occasionally, pleasantly extends the deceit and, when they reappear, can be appreciated with fresh eyes.

Paintings or posters suggestive of distant landscapes can be given a foreground of houseplants, as a modest *trompe l'oeil*; those mimicking windows, with painted shutters or mullions and frames, can be especially amusing in a room which would otherwise have dull or depressing views out. Hand-painted murals depicting leafy scenes are the ultimate permanent *trompe l'oeil*.

Trompe l'oeil

Plants feature heavily in this dramatic, painted perspective of a balcony and the landscape beyond. The potted geranium placed against the mural adds to the pleasant spatial confusion, being a typical balcony plant, as does fatsia on the table.

You can place a plant in front of a life-size painting of that type, for a little pun: a painting of lilies fronted by potted lilies, for example, or miniature roses in front of a collection of hand-tinted rose prints. You can add to the joke by propping the foreground accordingly; a dish filled with hummocks of moss or pine cones for a woodland image, for example, or a bowl of pot-pourri for a country cottage garden image.

Wallpaper with floral or foliar themes is an easy option: reproductions of the ornately lush eighteenth-century chintz types; the

simple wallpapers of the Arts and Crafts movement, as exemplified by William Morris; or E. Q. Nicholson's large-scale, realistic *Runner Beans* and *Fig Leaves* patterns of the 1950s. Tiny, sprig-type or mini-print leaf and flower patterns, however, 'read' as a tone or texture, rather than definable images. A whole room needn't be papered, just a single wall or panel. In a conservatory, for example, paper the solid wall with a floral or foliage-patterned wallpaper with a white background, to create the image of lush verdure at a stroke.

Oriental splendour

The two and three dimensional melt into one, with a *Cymbidium*, grass-green lampshades and artificial fruit in a Victorian bell jar backed by an Oriental mural.

This is obviously an expensive exercise but Oriental landscape prints, framed panels of wallpaper with an Oriental theme or Oriental posters could create a similar effect.

Plant Supports

Support can come from above or below, so stems can trail or climb and small or medium-sized plants can be closer to eye level, for extra stature and height, especially in plant groups without large specimens.

Bamboo poles, singly or in tripods, are traditional supports for climbers; if you cut your own bamboo, leave a few leaves to dry papery beige, for pleasing, flag-like decoration. Bare branches make natural-looking supports; some are flat and fan-shaped, rather like trellis – hazel often produces flat sprays – while others such as alder are more like miniature trees. Pussy willow with catkins; alder or larch with cones; old lichen-covered apple tree branches – a country walk after a storm or after forestry thinning can be very rewarding! For lightweight climbers, use dried teasel stems, complete with thistle heads, or dried angelica stems from the herb garden. Dead, sun-bleached aerial ivy roots are fantastically sculptural and make excellent supports. Large, tree-like houseplants can support climbers: a passionflower (*Passiflora caerulea*) through a weeping fig (*Ficus benjamina*), for example.

At garden centres, ignore the division between indoor and outdoor supports, especially since the former tend to be overpriced, weak and coy. For a formal effect, train climbers such as pink jasmine (*Jasminum polyanthum*) up and over an umbrella-like wire support used for standard weeping roses. For a really large-scale effect, sink the foundations of a lightweight, off-the-peg wire or wood trellis in two large flowerpots and train a climber up each side, to meet in the middle. Old-fashioned brushwood pea sticks, made of hazel, oak or chestnut trimmings, can be used to support indoor climbers.

For fun, train a climber over an old-fashioned dressmaker's model or easel, or place small plants on the rungs of a wooden or

Slightly surreal

△ An everyday ivy is given a setting of Baroque richness, with its pulpit-like table and built-in frame in rich blue fretwork, and glittery, gold-paper backdrop.

Single-stemmed supports are rather like tree trunks, especially effective supporting mound- or hummock-forming plants, which visually become the crown of the tree.

Pussy willow

◁ Bamboo canes, wire hoops, plastic trellis and green-dyed pea sticks are traditional plant supports – adequate but anonymous and unmemorable. This dried bulrush and freshly picked pussy willow provide support and sculptural interest to the flower stems of a moth orchid.

The bulrush and willow have been positioned and angled with the care given to an Oriental flower arrangement, which, in a sense, this is.

The raffia used to tie the stems to their supports is another 'design statement' – it becomes part of the display instead of reticent and mildly apologetic.

Spaced out

▷ Unlike the dense planting above, this tiered plant stand displays its contents in a more spacious, military-like way.

Red-flowered hibiscus and anthurium, white-flowered lily and hydrangea and a mound of green mind-your-own-business are interspersed with books.

The smaller plant stand contains a single mind-your-own-business.

metal stepladder and a trailing plant on the top platform. On a small scale, make three dimensional frames such as globes out of galvanized wire or flexible rattan canes.

Almost anything stable and level can support plants from below: tiny or elaborate plant stands, old sewing machine stands, stools or old wooden high chairs, for example. A pair from a row of old wooden school desks would make a fabulous basis for a plant grouping, with plants on the desks, seats and surrounding floor.

Tiered tracery

△ A three-tiered plant stand in black-painted wirework supports variegated ivy, creeping fig and white *Primula obconica*. Limiting the choice of plants and arranging them symmetrically creates a formal effect, emphasized by the pyramid-like hierarchy of the tiers themselves.

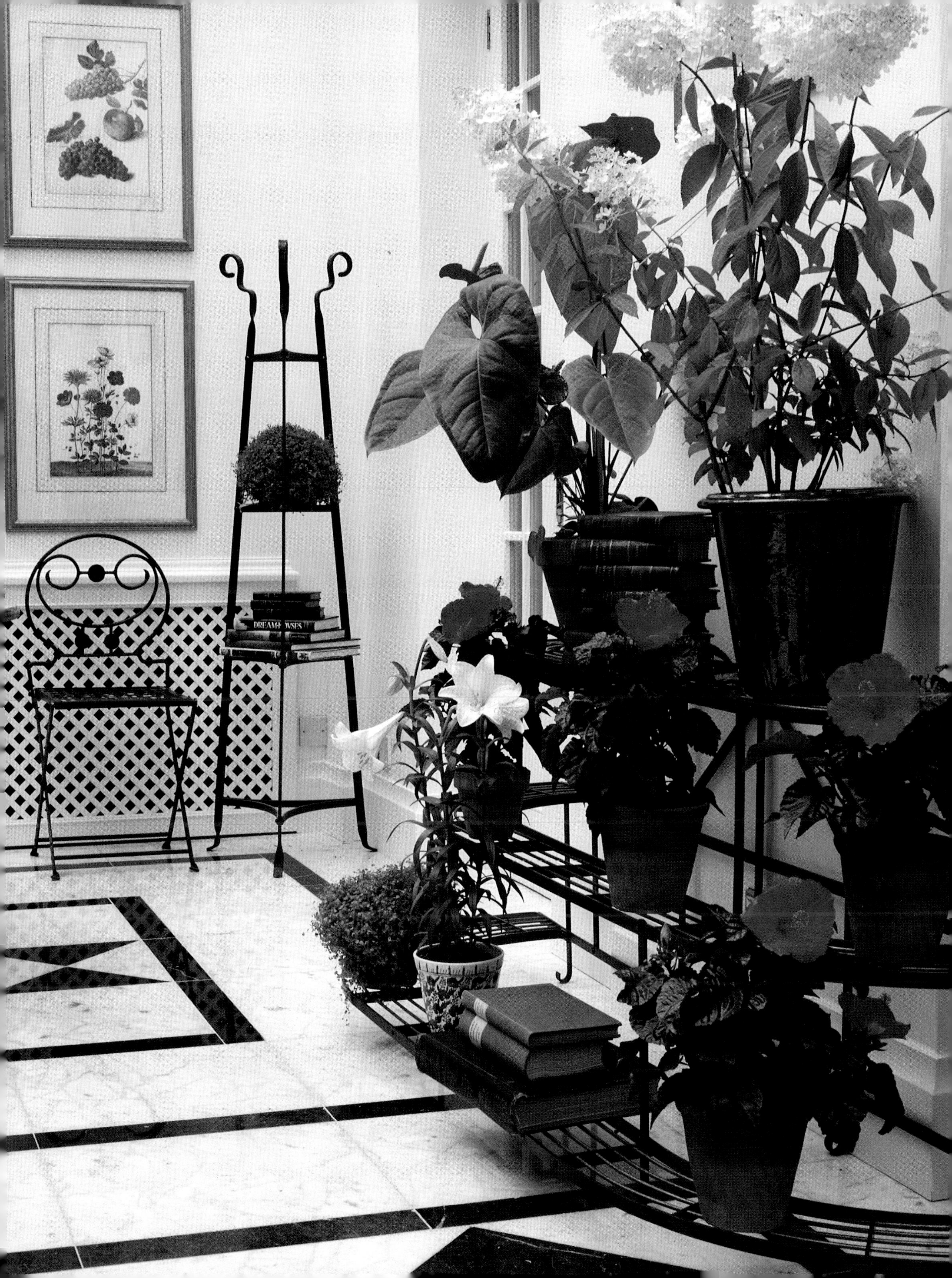
DREAMHOUSES

Decorative Mulches

With a houseplant in a prime position, such as on a dining table or coffee table, it is often worth concealing the potting compost with a more decorative mulch. For houseplants grouped in a basket or other large container, mulches can also conceal the flowerpot rims and spaces between the pots, creating a unified effect.

Mulches can be permanent or temporary. Permanent organic mulches include chipped bark, available in coarse and fine grades, and cocoa-bean shell shavings. Both are sold at garden centres, as are various grades of potting or horticultural grit, traditionally used for top-dressing cacti and succulents.

From builders' merchants come stone chippings, pebbles and sea-washed cobbles, in various sizes and colours. (Collecting your own attractive pebbles and cobbles from seaside holidays is a pleasant alternative source.) Specialist tropical-fish shops often carry a range of glass and marble chippings in natural and dyed colours, as well as tiny shells. Spread an evenly dense layer, leaving enough space between the surface and the pot rim for watering, but do not build a permanent mulch thickly around the stem or it may rot.

Semi-permanent organic mulches include various mosses, such as bun moss, with its velvety hummocks; sphagnum moss, bright green when fresh, slowly going rusty beige; and silvery grey reindeer moss. These can be ordered from a florist or collected from the wild. Packed tightly over the surface of the potting compost, moss can create the impression of a sward of green lawn in miniature.

As well as mulching the surface, you can build up layers of contrasting mulches in a transparent glass-sided container such as a fish

Mossy mulch

◁ Bun moss and smooth water-washed stones provide a life-like setting for spring crocus. Note the cut stems of tree ivy, adding to the outdoors imagery and contrasting with the cut rose prop.

Glass and glass

△ A transparent glass *cachepot* contains a single thickness of multi-coloured marbles which conceal a 'working' flowerpot. You can do the same with any wide-mouthed glass container.

bowl, battery jar or cylindrical vase, planted with hippeastrums or other bulbs, giving the fascinating effect of a geological cross section.

TEMPORARY MULCHES
Temporary mulches – say, for a dinner party centrepiece – can be almost anything that is pleasing to look at and comes in small units: fresh lawn clippings; dried pulses such as lentils or kidney beans; various pot-pourris; pine or larch cones; children's glass marbles; sugared almonds, or autumnal leaves, as they are from the garden or ironed between sheets of waxed paper for a glossy effect. Spread a layer of clingfilm between the potting compost and the decorative mulch, to keep the latter dry and clean, if necessary.

Paraphernalia

There is almost no limit to what you can put next to a houseplant to attract the eye. The balance of 'pulling power' ranges from an impressive plant or plant group visually punctuated by a tiny ornament to an impressive ornament or group of ornaments, visually punctuated by a tiny plant.

Animal figures and houseplants are great fun to mix and match. Ceramic, china, wooden, stone, glass or papier mâché sheep, pigs, horses, geese or cows can 'graze', singly or en masse, at the base of a houseplant or houseplant cluster. Facsimile frogs and toads, as in real life, can seek shade under the shelter of a large leaf; realistic, life-sized feathered birds, manufactured in the Far East, can alight (albeit permanently) on the branch of of a houseplant tree; duck decoys can nestle in a nest of houseplant foliage; stuffed owls in a Victorian glass belljar can peer out from a surrounding frame of greenery.

Depending on the scale, from diminutive, old-fashioned lead farmhouse animals to larger-than-life replicas; and the style, from representational to ethnic or modern, the effect can range from actual creatures in a dense jungle to a light-hearted bit of visual fantasy. (A densely plant-filled, deep window-sill with a sprinkling of animals can be endlessly fascinating.)

Caged songbirds are not everyone's moral ideal, but a setting of greenery is pleasant and adds to the fantasy of nature encapsulated and recreated indoors. Goldfish in a fishbowl nestled among houseplants is perhaps less controversial, but equally effective.

As a variation of the pun on relative scale, toy and model cars can contain plants or seemingly scoot round them; diminutive, wooden dolls' house furniture can be displayed with houseplants, or houseplants 'sit' on slightly larger dolls' furniture.

Figurines, whether Victorian fairings, carved-wood African statues, opalescent glass, Art deco gamines or highly stylized, saccharine china ladies in ballgowns, benefit from a leafy setting. Climbers can entwine a mass-produced terracotta or reconstituted stone bust (available relatively inexpensively from garden centres), or ethnic, wall-hung masks.

Trailing plants are especially effective weaving their way among a collection of small objects such as paperweights, ink or perfume bottles, salt and pepper containers, sugar shakers or fishpaste lids, knitting together the spaces between. Any display of cups and saucers, jugs, vases or jelly moulds, is enlivened if a few actually contain a suitably sized plant. If you collect boxes – porcupine-quill boxes popular during the Raj, for example, or tea caddies – display some open, with plants inside, others empty and shut.

Last, cheap, naff architectural souvenirs – plastic Eiffel Towers, pyramids, Tower of Londons or Empire State Buildings – are fun in a setting of houseplant greenery, however inaccurate in scale and reality.

Sweet dreams

A folk-art statue of a sleeping boy, his head resting on a gourd cushion, becomes the dreamy focal point in a table-top grove of mixed houseplants. The combination creates an exotic, foreign, slightly surreal mood, like the paintings of Henri Rousseau.

The fat cactus visually balances the cushion, repeating its global shape and the palm-like, arching Madagascar dragon tree adds a jungly reference.

Collecting paraphernalia for propping plants, whether having the wherewithal to shop in top antique stores or ferreting out unloved treasure from other people's junk and jumble, garage and car boot sales, is in the blood. Some people are just better at it than others.

Foreign craft and gift shops, whether Indian, Oriental, South American or African, are delightful hunting grounds, especially if you can't face browsing through second-hand flotsam and jetsam.

Fabrics

Fabrics let you change a houseplant's immediate setting at a stroke, whether to simplify it, so that the plant's silhouette and shadows are more easily seen; or to add richness and intricacy and via two dimensions, the implication of three-dimensional flowers and foliage.

Fabrics can be used vertically and horizontally. The simple, solid-colour linen placemat that picks up the flower colour of an African violet resting on it and simultaneously frames the plant, seen from above; the Liberty-print curtains that add background floral colour to a foreground of foliage houseplants; the lace doily beneath a maidenhair fern that repeats its delicacy; the bright yellow Provençal print fabric that enwraps a flowerpot of yellow chrysanthemums or daffodils; or the gathered Paisley shawl, with its curled teardrop pattern based on an unfurling date palm frond, that surrounds the base of a potted palm; all add to the impact and mood of a houseplant. Natural raw silk, dramatic jungle prints or polite, traditional floral chintz fabric can be stretched over wooden frames and hung as panels on the wall behind a group of houseplants, to draw attention to their presence. Panels of wallpaper can be used in the same way.

Interesting scarves or remnants can be temporarily draped round flowerpots or tied, neckerchief-fashion. For one-night spectaculars, generous lengths of metallic fabric or just immaculate white sheeting or natural muslin, could be wrapped, bunting-fashion, around the flowerpots of large, specimen houseplant trees. A square scarf or fabric circle, cut with pinking shears, can be brought up and over a flowerpot, and fixed with a rubber band, to create a softly pleated, instant *cachepot* with a frilly neck ruffle. Old bow ties can be tied round the rim of a flowerpot, for a slightly formal, slightly humorous, Magritte-like touch, and though crochetwork toilet-paper covers

Visual pun

△ Miniature roses in their straw basket seem to grow, as a natural extension, from the intensely beautiful and slightly sculptural floral tapestry fabric on which they sit.

Careful watering is essential for plants displayed on a fabric base.

Centre stage

▷ Softly pleated, large-check gingham, glued to the inner rim of plastic pots and finished with self bows, is used to make matching *cachepots* for a trio of double narcissi.

This is a studio shot – note the non-matching curtains and blank landscape beyond – but colour-co-ordinating fabric *cachepot*, wallpaper, curtains and houseplants is a real option.

are considered the ultimate kitsch, brightly or subtly coloured knitted or crochetwork flowerpot covers might be fun – simple patterns for the beginner, Arran or Fair-Isle knit for the more advanced.

Unwanted 'boob tubes' can be pulled up the sides of a largish plastic flowerpot, as a jokey fabric sleeve; hemmed sections of brightly coloured stretch leg warmers, up smaller pots. And all the panoply of embellishments – sequins, rhinestones, buttons, beads,

appliqué motifs, fringe, gold studs, rhinestone pins, silk flowers, feathers – that belong to the world of fashion can be called into play, for a light-hearted finishing touch.

For a more permanent, 'serious' effect, fabric can be saturated with PVA adhesive, four parts adhesive to one part water, and glued to a plastic flowerpot to create a *cachepot*, in which a smaller, plant-filled flowerpot fits. The fabric can hug the pot tightly, or loosely swathe it to create a generous, pleated,

turban-like sculptured effect, with one end diagonally overlapping the other. Allow for turning over the fabric on the lower edge and returning the fabric well over the upper rim; for a turban-like effect, you need a rectangle one and a half times the rim's diameter, times twice the pot's height, plus turnovers. Use rubber gloves for the exercise; once the fabric is in position, gently tack it with drawing pins or thumb tacks to the inside rim while it dries over a radiator or in an airing cupboard.

Seasonal Themes

Houseplants at Christmas

THIS IS A three-pronged challenge. Permanent houseplants with no festive associations at all – even the lowly rubber plant – can become attractive Christmas features; temporary winter houseplants, often short-lived and small, can be displayed creatively; and it is possible to borrow wholesale from the garden.

Any substantial, woody-stemmed houseplant is a potential Christmas tree, hung with decorations. Use American red-and-white-striped candy canes, foil-covered Santa Clauses or bags of foil-covered chocolate coins; fake icicles, Christmas baubles, bells and balls; red, green, silver, gold or white ribbon bows; miniature artificial fruit; glass or wooden angels or animals; metallic stars, tinsel or beads; 'pearl' ropes; wired-up kumquats, small clementines or spray-painted walnuts or pine cones; or gingerbread cookies.

Weeping figs are especially suitable and Christmas-tree lights can be strung through the branches. Palms and palm-like Madagascar dragon trees (*Dracaena marginata*) or corn palms (*Dracaena fragrans*) can sport 'crops' of metallic-painted nuts or fake fruit tightly clustered under the leaves or hung on various lengths of fine black cotton.

Trailing or arching plants such as kangaroo vines, spider plant or asparagus ferns can similarly be 'done up' for Christmas, with baubles all along the length of the stems. You can

Seasonal spectacular

Here, boundaries between houseplants and interior design are blurred, with a drinks table transformed into a woodland in miniature. Dwarf conifers dislike winter warmth, so a cool entrance hall would be ideal; otherwise, once festivities are over, give the plants a day or two in a cool room, then move them outdoors. Or, use houseplant 'trees' such as ming aralia (*Polyscias fruticosa*) or instant 'trees' made from branches stuck into pots. For more obvious Christmas imagery, add mistletoe or Christmas-tree baubles.

Conical dwarf conifers such as Chamaecyparis,
*   Picea or Abies cultivars*
Dwarf bamboo or ornamental grass
Thyme or heather
Ivy or cut stems of ivy
Bun moss or mossy stones
Mixed conifer sprigs or twigs
White gravel
Natural pebbles
Candles
Silver-covered almonds or silver sprayed pebbles
Large, foil-covered stones

1 Place the tallest conifer at the back, off centre, then a slightly shorter one in front. Add a thyme or heather and a taller bamboo or grassy-leaved plant to one side, in a rough, 'L'-shaped layout. Tuck an ivy or ivy stems to one side, overhanging the edge.
2 Using large clumps of bun moss or mossy stones, conceal the pots. Use more moss to form a curving, velvety bank and tuck in mixed conifer sprigs or twigs. Place smaller outcrops of bun moss and a few large, foil-covered stones here and there.
3 Cover one side of the table with white gravel. Make outcrops of natural-coloured gravel and silvered almonds, tucked in crevices between mounds of bun moss, and on top of the moss.
4 On the other side, place candles and glasses, drinks, hors-d'oeuvres or decorations such as the eggs and Cellophane parcels shown.

extend the decorations to include the supports – tying metallic balls or ribbon bows on trellis, for example, or topping a bamboo pole wigwam with a Christmas tree fairy or star.

Rest miniature metallic balls in the centre of an African violet or peanut cactus or on the spines of a larger cactus. Place a single, large Christmas-tree ball or cluster in the raised centre of the rosette-forming plant, or tuck tiny balls, here and there, into the base. Make sequin waste bow ties and tuck these round the base of aspidistra, mother-in-law's tongue or other erect houseplants.

Spray paint dried hydrangeas, teasels or honesty, or silver dollar, (*Lunaria annua*) seed heads, silver or gold and insert them in the base of a mound- or clump-shaped foliage houseplant, such as a fern. Alternatively, insert branches of contorted willow or hazel in the centre, and decorate as above. Bulk out a dull green foliage plant with variegated ivy or holly sprigs, mistletoe, eucalyptus sprigs or berried twigs of pyracantha or cotoneaster.

Certain seasonal houseplants coincide with Christmas: poinsettias, winter cherries, Christmas peppers, Christmas heathers, azaleas, cyclamens, kalenchoes, polyanthus, Christmas cacti and forced paperwhite narcissi and hyacinths. The larger the plants are, or the more you have of any one sort, the easier it is to make something of them. Single small plants can look half-hearted; try placing one in a large brandy snifter or a dish filled with moss, silver tinsel or metallic Christmas tree ropes. Or you could fill the container with gold or silver beads, or even sugared almonds. You could also rest a small plant in a little metallic paper gift bag, the flowerpot propped on crumpled newspaper, if necessary, and the top of the bag filled with moss. Several small houseplants can be displayed temporarily in a gift box, its lid propped open or removed and the space between the plants filled with moss or crumpled tissue paper in toning colours.

Use a cluster of small Christmas houseplants

to create the setting for miniature Nativity scenes – perhaps not accurate in terms of Bethlehem's flora, but fun none the less.

If you are making or buying a door wreath, make an extra one, lay it horizontally on a table and fill the centre with little houseplants, set on a plate with the spaces between covered in moss. You can incorporate candles into the display, as well.

Wrap flexible artificial conifer garlands (popular in America) round a plastic flowerpot or group of flowerpots, using double-sided tape, to make a conifer nest. Interweave

Stop and go

Poinsettias combine in one plant the two traditional colours of Christmas – red and green – although they are now available in creamy white and pink forms.

Large, specimen poinsettias such as these are stunning, but smaller plants benefit from grouping, either with other poinsettias or as part of a mixed planting dish. Alternatively, gently rest them, pot and all, in the centre of a big jug or vase of conifer or ivy foliage or mixed greenery, including sprigs of holly in berry, another Christmas symbol.

Top quality fake poinsettia blooms can be inserted into any dense foliage houseplant, even the Boston fern shown here in the fireplace, to 'festivize' it.

sprigs of ivy or artificial, wired ivy among the conifer, for interest.

Set a white-flowered poinsettia in a large bowl or *cachepot* and cover the potting compost with creamy white dried ornamental gourds; for a red-flowered plant, use lacquer-covered polystyrene apples, with cranberries as infill, perhaps first painted with egg white then sprinkled with caster sugar, for a frosted effect. Alternatively, wrap miniature 'fun-size' boxes of candy in pretty metallic paper and ribbon bows to tone with the flowers, and pile these Christmas 'gifts' on the compost. (With

all of these, water the plants from beneath!)

Pot-grown conifers from garden centres can make temporary houseplants, ideally for cool rooms or halls. Quite large, quick-growing hedging conifers are relatively cheap; decorate as above. Temporarily borrow a potted bay, box, *Euonymus*, *Fatsia*, x *Fatshedera* or spotted laurel from a patio and bring it indoors for Christmas. Alternatively, decorate such plants, *in situ*, with waterproof decorations, to celebrate Christmas in the garden as well as the house, perhaps co-ordinating the decorations with the door wreath.

Houseplants at Easter

For many, Easter is an important religious occasion, but more generally, it is a celebration of spring. For children, it is a joyous holiday, with chocolate bunnies, decorated eggs and Easter egg hunts on the lawn. Houseplant displays can reflect this spectrum, from devout to delightful.

White lilies symbolize the serious side of Easter. Displayed with a backdrop of bare branches – hazel (*Corylus avellana*) or Pekin willow (*Salix matsudana* 'Tortuosa'), for example – or even in a twiggy outer basket, they convey the dual theme of death and rebirth, as do tight groups of cut Easter lilies or arum lilies (*Zantedeschia aethiopica*), foliage houseplants and bare branches.

For fun, fill wicker Easter baskets with primroses or violets dug up from the garden and cover the soil surface with sphagnum or bun moss, then scatter tiny, foil-covered eggs on top, or buy pots of dwarf narcissi, polyanthus or hyacinths and use them instead.

Purples

Easter and spring melt together in many minds, and spring displays such as these violets, polyanthus, pansies and forget-me-nots are as welcome as more obvious, Easter floral imagery.

Easter eggs

Dyed Easter eggs nestle in a miniature lawn – grass seed sprouted in a shallow dish. Try using foil-wrapped chocolate or wooden eggs, mustard and cress sprouts or sections of bun moss instead.

Another variation on the egg theme are plant-filled eggshells. After carefully removing the contents of soft-boiled eggs, fill the shells with peat-based potting compost and tiny plants such as individual stems of peanut cactus (*Chamaecereus sylvestrî*) or club moss (*Selaginella* species). Display the eggs in egg cups or an open egg box, painted a pastel tint.

For props, build up a rabbit collection – china, wicker, glass, marble, wood or stone – and set them among a forest of foliage houseplants or 'grazing' in a shallow, moss-filled dish. Decorative eggs, too, can be had in a wide range of materials and styles, from cheerful, folk-art Russian nest eggs, one inside another, to elegant eggs made of semi-precious stones such as onyx or amethyst. Place large ones individually among plants or fill a transparent bowl with small ones, which can also be used as solid, decorative mulches.

Last, you can make an 'Easter tree' by hanging small decorative eggs and tiny wicker, egg-filled baskets on the branches of a weeping fig (*Ficus benjamina*).

Tip
Keep lilies and other flowering bulbs as cool as possible, to extend the display period.

Houseplants in the Garden

Think of your house as a semi-permeable membrane, with houseplants moving in both directions according to season. In spring and summer, when you are likely to spend more time in the garden anyway, houseplants can enhance permanent garden planting or beautify a bare patio, and also benefit from improved health, as rain helps wash away winter grime and fresh air keeps pests such as whitefly at bay. In autumn, refreshed after a summer outdoors, they can be moved in again.

Some houseplants such as ivy (*Hedera* species and varieties) and the closely related fatsia (*Fatsia japonica*) are attractive all year round, indoors or out. Tender houseplants can stay days, weeks or months outdoors between the last frost in spring and the first in autumn. A patio table can then be treated as dining-room table, with a houseplant, houseplant group or miniature garden as a centrepiece. Patio walls can be fitted with Continental-style metal brackets to hold pots of geraniums and other houseplants; trolleys, layered with houseplants and moved from place to place, for even exposure to light.

Line out houseplants along the coping of a low brick wall, making sure first that they are heavy enough not to be blown over and, should they be, that no danger to people can result. Otherwise, fix window boxes or wooden plant troughs to the top of the wall and rest the plants in them.

Fill a sheltered, shady garden spot with tender ferns such as bird's-nest fern (*Asplenium nidus avis*), brake fern (*Pteris* species and varieties) and Boston fern (*Nephrolepis exaltalta* 'Bostoniensis'); Cape primroses (*Streptocarpus* hybrids) and foliage begonias such as *B. rex*,

Tulips on parade

THIS AUTUMN PROJECT, taking less than ten minutes to prepare, can enliven your house for weeks on end in spring, at a fraction of the cost of a ready-made florist's display.

*Dwarf double early tulip bulbs, such as the orange-
  yellow 'Marechal Niel', the rosy pink 'Peach
  Blossom' or the scarlet 'Oranje Nassau'*
Fresh sphagnum moss
Small twigs, such as hazel or birch
Copper fish kettle
Bulb fibre
*Drainage material, such as pebbles or pieces of
  broken terracotta flowerpot*

1 Place a 2.5cm (1in) layer of drainage material at the bottom of the container, followed by a layer of moistened bulb fibre.

2 Plant the bulbs close together but not touching, with the tips just above the surface of the fibre, and a 2.5cm (1in) gap between the surface and the rim of the container.

3 Place in a dark spot, at a temperature of 0–7°C (32–45°F). Cold, dark conditions are essential for healthy root development. In a bright room, enclose the container in a black polythene bag. Keep the bulb fibre barely moist.

3 When 5–7.5cm (2–3in) of leaves are showing (usually 8–10 weeks after planting) gradually expose the plants to a little more warmth and light – an unheated spare room is ideal. Continue watering and keep below 14°C (60°F) until the flower buds are as high as the foliage.

4 Cover the bulb fibre with fresh sphaghum moss and insert twigs into the fibre to form a small, interwoven 'fence' around the rim, and move to the final display position.

PRACTICAL HINT
The flowers will last longer in a cool room than a hot one. Remember to water regularly and mist spray the sphagnum moss, to help it retain its green colour.

B. boweri and *B.* 'Cleopatra'. Given regular watering, feeding and occasional misting, fronds and leaves will grow large and lush by the time autumn comes. Cacti, succulents and waxy, grey and furry-leaved plants such as the cobweb houseleek (*Sempervivum arachnoideum*) and white velvet (*Tradescantia sillamontana*) thrive in a hot sunny garden spot, which encourages colour, waxiness and hairiness to intensify, as a protection against the light.

Use the garden itself as a propagating unit and nursery for houseplants, while displaying them at the same time. In late spring plant plantlets of spider plant (*Chlorophytum comosum* 'Vittatum') or mother of thousands (*Saxifraga stolonifera* 'Variegata') in moist, rich soil or potting compost in pots, bedding schemes or

mixed borders. Divide established houseplants of variegated ivy or the unusual ground ivy, (*Glechoma hederacea* 'Variegata', syn. *Nepeta hederacea* 'Variegata'), with its trailing stems of scalloped, round, white-edged leaves, into several small rooted sections. Both are ideal for summer hanging baskets, pots and tubs and by autumn each young plant will have itself grown substantial and they can be potted up and taken indoors, given as gifts or discarded.

TIP
Avoid drastic temperature changes by gradually exposing plants to higher or lower temperatures, over a few days. A well-lit garage or unheated room is usually a good 'decompression chamber'.

Snowdrops for winter cheer

DORMANT SNOWDROP BULBS can be temperamental and fail for no obvious reason, so snowdrops are traditionally increased by lifting and dividing established clumps immediately after flowering. This display calls for clumps of snowdrops, but you can easily 'cheat', courtesy of your local florist!

Clumps of snowdrop in bud
Fresh ivy leaves
Bulb fibre or loam or peat-based potting compost
Drainage material, such as pebbles or broken
    pieces of terracotta flowerpots
Fresh sphagnum moss
Woven twig basket
Colourful autumn leaves, such as maple or beech

1 Dig up snowdrop clumps, using a trowel or hand fork. Try to choose plants with compact leaves and short, sturdy flower stalks, and dig deeply, to get as much of the roots as possible.

2 Place a layer of drainage material in the bottom of the basket, then a layer of potting compost or bulb fibre. Plant the snowdrops to the same depth that they were in the garden, adjusting the level of the potting compost or bulb fibre as necessary, to cover the lower white portions of leaves and stalks.

3 Cover with a layer of sphagnum moss, decorated with ivy leaves, autumnal leaves and a few water-washed pebbles. Place in a cool, brightly lit spot and keep the potting compost or bulb fibre barely moist, mist spraying the moss from time to time. When the last snowdrops have faded, you can then replant them in the garden.

CUT FLOWER ALTERNATIVE

For a short-lived but equally beautiful display, buy bunches of cut snowdrops from your florist. Place them upright, together with an ivy leaf, in narrow, water-filled glasses, 1-2.5cm (½–1in) shorter than the depth of the basket. Place the glasses in the basket, filling the spaces between with sphagnum moss, potting compost or even scrunched-up bits of newspaper. Cover the surface with fresh sphagnum moss, as before, and place the leaves and pebbles in position. Top up the water daily and when the flowers fade, replace with fresh.

Spring forward

Grape hyacinths can be dug up from the garden in bud in spring and carefully potted up, or gently forced, planted as bulbs in flowerpots or bulb bowls in autumn and kept in cool, bright conditions.

Here, they are propped with dead winter leaves as a naturalistic touch, much as they might be in the garden.

Pot et Fleur

Fresh Flower Pot et Fleur

POT ET FLEUR is French for pot and flower, and refers to the traditional decorative practice of combining cut flowers with houseplants in a single, unified display. As a decorative technique, it brilliantly solves several style problems at once. First, often florists' cut foliage such as awkwardly shaped cypress or box sprigs actually detract from flowers, while top-class florists' foliage such as bear-grass eucalyptus or leatherleaf fern can be costly. Second, many popular cut flowers such as long-stemmed roses, chrysanthemums and carnations have no foliage when sold or foliage that is unappealing, and benefit from 'borrowed' foliage camouflage. And third, houseplants such as the peace lily, or *Spathyphyllum wallisii*; and queen's tears, or *Billbergia nutans* are dull-looking when not in flower, and even foliage houseplants such as ivy can be enhanced with 'borrowed' flowers.

The potential for creativity is virtually unlimited and botanical accuracy is completely irrelevant. Rather like illustrations in children's books, which allow the reader to combine the head of one animal with the body of another and the feet of yet a third, there is nothing to stop you combining the striking, strap-like leaves of an out-of-season *Clivia miniata* with a cluster of long-stemmed lilies, for example; exotic *Strelitzia regina*, or bird-of-paradise, flowers or a combination of both, inserted in

the centre of the leaf rosette. On a smaller scale but equally charming would be a cluster of cut miniature roses or multi-coloured freesias peeping out from the velvety foliage of the eyelash begonia, *Begonia boweri*. And even ordinary mixed bunches of flowers take on a 'designer' look, displayed within a setting of houseplant foliage.

With fresh flowers, normal conditioning procedures apply: re-cutting stems before inserting in a container of water, to which a few drops of bleach are added, to prevent a build-up of bacteria. Proprietary cut-flower food contains antibacterial agents, and can also be used. Re-cut the stems every few days,

82

Flowers and scents

◁ Cut lilies and gypsophila form the central feature of this spring fireplace display, surrounded by potted hydrangeas and fronted with a pot of the deliciously peppermint-scented, furry-leaved *Pelargonium tomentosum*.

Gypsophila dries naturally and can be left in situ, and the lilies replaced with fresh, or other flowers, as mood dictates.

Country fresh

▷ A wild, woolly mixture of scented-leaved and ivy-leaved pelargoniums (both in need of cutting back!), variegated ivy, stephanotis and cacti surround a container of cut daisies, for an informal *pot et fleur*.

The floral motif of the shell-covered *cachepot* adds another texture and dimension.

top up with fresh water and mist spray in warm, dry conditions.

You can insert the stems in cigar tubes, orchid tubes (narrow, round-bottomed glass or plastic vials) or empty glass food jars, hidden among the houseplant foliage and tied to small pea sticks inserted in the potting compost for stability, if necessary. You can also rest whole, small arrangements in saturated florist's foam block, among the leaves; or simply take the easy way out: surround an ordinary jar or vase of cut flowers with a ruff or landscape of foliage houseplants surrounding the base. Always replace faded flowers with fresh, or remove the container when finished.

SIMPLE CUT-FLOWER AND
HOUSEPLANT MINI-RECIPES

Singapore orchids with Boston fern (*Nephrolepis exaltata* 'Bostoniensis')
Gerberas with *Begonia rex*
Anemones with cyclamen
Turk's head ranunculus with *Asparagus sprengeri*
Iris with queen's tears (*Billbergia nutans*)
Freesias with hare's-foot fern (*Davallia canarienses*)
Chincherinchee with foxtail fern (*Asparagus meyeri*)
Miniature roses with eyelash begonia (*Begonia boweri*)
Spray carnations with scented-leaved geraniums such as *Pelargonium tomentosum*
Spray chrysanthemums with azalea
Tulips with angels' wings (*Caladium hortulanum* hybrids)
Lily-of-the-valley with club moss (*Selaginella* species)

Fake Flower Pot et Fleur

Fabric fake flowers, in the design world, have come in from the cold, and some are now so convincing that it is difficult, even at close range, to tell them apart from fresh flowers. The best are imported from the Far East, and made of silk or polyester; it is sensible to buy top-quality ones, even if it takes time to build up a good collection. The foliage attached to fake flowers can be disappointing and in many cases is best removed. Again, the unnatural-looking stems benefit from the camouflage of fresh houseplant foliage. Like dried flowers, they need no water and can be inserted directly in the potting compost, and can remain indefinitely.

You can use any of the 'recipes' given on page 83, or try your own: a cluster of fake delphiniums, for example, towering above a basal mass of kangaroo vine, or *Cissus antartica*; fake nasturtiums tucked into a trailing ivy; or fake scabious, with their country-garden charm, enlivening a worthy but otherwise boring cast-iron plant, *Aspidistra elatior*.

Fake flowers that don't pretend to be anything other than fake include old-fashioned feather flowers, the most subtle made from natural pheasant or partridge feathers but also available in bright dyed colours. Coleus, with their slightly bizarre, Victorian colours and own insignificant flowers could be given a bit of pzazz with the addition of pheasant or partridge feather flowers. Of a similar type are all the hand-crafted shell flowers, leather flowers, nylon-tights-over-coathanger-wire flowers, beadwork flowers and corn-husk flowers, which are reminiscent of a former, gentler and more leisurely time, and can add intrigue to featureless houseplants.

Cheating in style

△ Lifelike pink and yellow silk freesias enliven an *Aglaonema*, or Chinese evergreen, and *Syngonium*, or goosefoot plant. Freesia itself is rarely grown as a houseplant, partly because its own leaves are so unruly. Though purists might see this as tampering with nature, there's no reason why you can't make any foliage houseplant into a 'flowering' one, either with its own fake flowers when out of season or, as here, frankly borrowed.

In the pink

◁ Real African violets and their delicately sprigged *cachepot* set the mood and provide the colour theme for a mixture of fake cut flowers including sweet peas, lilac and China aster, in tones of pink and purple, as well as a fake weeping fig.

A collection of mixed colour African violets could be displayed clustered round the base of a vase, for variation in height and scale – African violets, perhaps more than other collectors' plants, can look artificial seen in large numbers.

Leaves, Berries and Branches

All sorts of cut-plant material can augment houseplants, as *pot et fleur* displays in spirit, even if not technically flowers. Combining clusters of small houseplants around a central 'fountain' of cut branches of bay, tree ivy, for example, or pittosporum foliage, can turn disparate items into a coherent feature. (Glossy-leaved evergreen foliage such as bay, tree ivy and pittosporum, provided the leaves are mature, will remain fresh and unwilted for hours out of water, so you can use them horizontally, as a temporary foreground or 'nest' round a flowerpot or group of flowerpots.) A big vase of mixed foliage, perhaps including variegated and coloured-leaved garden foliage, can be a similar keystone for a cluster of houseplants. Or you could tuck in the centre, pot and all, a colourful, small bromeliad such as *Neoregelia carolinae tricolor*, with its yellow and green variegated, red-centred leaf rosette, as a flower-like focal point.

On a smaller scale, little jugs of golden or plain green privet-hedge clippings can be interspersed among small houseplants, for a 'mix and match' display.

Rich brown glycerined sprays of beech or chestnut foliage can add bulk and subtle contrast to a collection of coloured foliage plants. In winter, bare branches can be just as effective: hazel, with its catkins; alder, with its black bark and male catkins and female fruits; birch, with its elegant, lacy branchlets. Bizarre rather than natural-looking are the twisted, contorted branches of Pekin willow, *Salix matsudana* 'Tortuosa' and contorted hazel, *Corylus avellana* 'Contorta'.

Woodland vignette

This columnnar *pot et fleur* comprises all things green: various mosses and ferns with a sprinkling of grass attached, Solomon's seal, its green berries replacing the delicate, white, lily-of-the-valley flowers that precede them, and a pine branch. Though specific ingredients are listed, particular proportions or ingredients matter less than the over-all finished effect. The display only just qualifies as a *pot et fleur*, since the ferns have roots, but is relatively short lived – a fun item for a fun occasion.

Saturated florist's foam block
Florist's mastic
Florist's prong
Base
Hairpins or U-shaped wires
Bun moss
Reindeer moss
Sphagnum moss
Solomon's seal (Polygonatum)
Polypody fern (Polypodium vulgare)
Male fern (Dryopteris felix mas)
Pine branch

1 Using a sharp knife, cut off one, long side of the block to form a square section, then slice off the corners to form a column, roughly circular in section.
2 Place a florist's mastic cross in the middle of the base and press a florist's prong on top. Up-end the column and impale it on the prong.
3 Starting from the bottom, build up a dense covering of green moss, impaling the pieces to the column with fine wire hairpins or U-shaped pins.
4 Turn the column slowly as you proceed, for an evenly dense covering. Add occasional clumps of fern, pinning their rootstock to the foam block and covering the roots with moss, to keep them damp.
5 Insert pine or other interesting twiggy branches, to balance the ferns. Insert the Solomon's seal stem so it arches over the column, and finally, press small pieces of silvery grey reindeer moss here and there.

Room by Room

Entrance Halls

ENTRANCE HALLS, LIKE bathrooms, are often compact, transitional spaces with varying degrees of light and warmth. Unlike bathrooms, halls are the gateway to a home and meant to give a flavour of things to come. Small, single plants rarely have impact; here, the challenge is to create a feeling of floral and foliar bulk in a limited space.

CHOICE OF PLANTS
If possible, use large, vertical specimens such as palm, a favourite Victorian hall plant; fiddleleaf fig (*Ficus lyrata*) or shade tolerant false palms: *Dracaena marginata* or *Dracaena fragrans*. Tough ferns such as holly fern (*Cyrtomium falcatum*), rabbit's-foot fern (*Davallia canariensis*) or asparagus ferns (*Asparagus* species), and mother-in-law's tongue (*Sansevieria* species) and cast iron plant (*Aspidistra elatior*) are medium-sized, long-term plants tolerant of hall conditions. All can be grouped with short-term, seasonal plants – high-key pink azaleas, for example, or pristine white pot chrysanthemums.

A hall is ideal for *pot et fleur*: a jug of tree ivy in berry, for example, to pad out a group of small houseplants. Cut branches or seasonal flowers from the front garden displayed in a hall emphasize its transitional role between house and garden, or pots of the same variety of plant such as camellia, Canterbury bells or marguerites displayed inside and outside the front door, and alternated every few days, to refresh the plants inside and extend the season of display.

CHOICE OF POSITIONS
The hall table is the traditional location for plants but shelves can also present compact plants close to or at eye-level height; triangular, built-in corner shelves, for example, or glass shelves in a hall window. Plant-filled baskets can be hung at various heights in front of a hall window; a windowed stair landing can become a mini-conservatory, with hanging baskets and floor-level plants intermingling. Fill high stairwells with hanging plants (provided you can reach them for maintenance) or a single, specimen tree; train ivy up a newelpost or bannisters as a lighthearted alternative to moss poles. Grow a vigorous climber such as grape ivy (*Rhoicissus rhomboidea*) or hoya (*Hoya carnosa*) around a framed mirror, painting or print above a hall table, as an additional, living frame.

CHOICE OF STANDS AND CONTAINERS
Short plants can be elevated on bamboo or

Foliage fountain

◁ A Boston fern on a narrow bamboo plant stand makes use of an odd, 'leftover' corner at the top of a stairwell. The greenery contrasts with the architectural form of the bannisters and acts as a visual punctuation point.

Like most ferns, Boston fern prefers filtered light.

Compact jungle

▷ Plants and birds combine to create a hallway jungle in miniature. The circular staircase provides the permanent framework for a boisterous grape ivy, interspersed with 'ordinary' ivy.

The collection of tables and chests make attractive plant stands, featuring a large, green-and-white variegated dumb cane, and a cluster of smaller plants including maidenhair fern, castor oil plant, fatsia and philodendron.

wirework plant stands or *jardinières*. Umbrella stands, chimney pots, wicker dustbins or even sturdy wire mesh netting tubes make jokey, alternative plant pedestals. A simple bentwood or metal folding chair could hold a substantial plant. Free-standing bentwood coat racks can support hanging baskets as can coat hooks or old-fashioned wooden clothes pegs.

On tables or shelves, standardizing small containers, if several are used, helps unify a display; containers can be part of the display, especially if based on a single theme, like wicker baskets or white Parianware.

A large moss basket can be filled with pots of forced bulbs, cinerarias, primulas or cyclamen; the 'borrowed' greenery of the basket increases the impression of foliage. In a country-style entrance hall, fill a wooden trug or wicker basket with small densely packed houseplants, their pots concealed with moss; an upturned boater or floppy straw hat could be similarly filled with houseplants and moss.

Enclosed glass containers, such as Ward cases, protect delicate plants from hall draughts and accidental knocks and give them added visual presence.

Living Rooms

Often the largest room in the house and the one most on public show, a living room offers maximum opportunities for houseplant display. Substantial, sculptural plants can find a home here and provide large-scale drama, especially if well lit, while collections of diminutive plants can enliven a corner table top. Medium-sized plants can be used to punctuate visually bookcases, shelves, desks and other surfaces.

CHOICE OF PLANTS

The choice is virtually limitless, though the year-round warmth and dry atmosphere in most living rooms tend to favour tender plants and make short shrift of hardy, temperate-climate ones such as azaleas and spring bulbs. Most effective is a permanent framework of tough, tolerant foliage houseplants such as palms, kangaroo vine (*Cissus antarctica*) and asparagus ferns (*Asparagus* species and varieties), as a backdrop for come-and-go, seasonal flowering plants and cut flowers, *pot et fleur* fashion.

The living room and large specimen plant (see pages 18–21), deserve each other, in the nicest possible way: the former provides the space and attractive background; the latter provides a focal point and character. Tightly clustered foliage houseplant groups, such as large, floor-level corner displays can be equally

effective and form the stage setting for seasonal cut branches such as wands of pussy willow or forced flowering cherry or fake or fresh flowers. Fresh flowers a little past their best can often do another brief tour of duty tucked in with foliage plants in a large-scale, floor-level, living-room display; the heavy pollen and slightly papery or faded petals that give away a flower's age seen up close, are not apparent seen from a safe distance.

Extravagant houseplants, whether in terms of cost or beauty − bird of paradise (*Strelitzia reginae*), for example, flamingo flower (*Anthurium scherzianum*) or hippeastrums (*Hippeastrum* hybrids) − merit the centre-stage setting of a living room and provide 'conversation pieces', so valued by interior designers.

A study in greens

(*overleaf*)
Healthy foliage plants need no apology or 'heightening' with flowers. Here, variegated ivies, weeping figs, *Dracaena fragans massangeana*, palm and *Sparmannia africana* or house lime visually soften the plain white walls and polished wooden floor. The house lime is the 'odd plant out', bearing, as it does, small yellow-stamened white flowers in spring and early summer, as a bonus to its handsome leaves.

Formal symmetry

▽ Fireplaces are inherently symmetrical and using plants symmetrically is a natural response. Here, a pair of shade-tolerant, mother-in-law's tongue or snakeskin plant (*Sansevieria trifasciata laurentii*) is partnered with bulrush-filled vases on the mantelpiece.

It is one of the most tolerant houseplants, vulnerable only to overwatering and low temperatures in winter.

High key, low key

◁ Hippeastrums in palest pink create a dramatic focal point against a rich, dark setting based on scarlet, deep green and brown − an unlikely colour combination but one that 'works'.

Hippeastrums are almost immoral in their splendour, and watching the snake-like stems and buds develop gives child-like pleasure to people of any age. This, coupled with the ease of getting bulbs to flower first time, makes them eminently popular, and dormant bulbs are marketed in gift boxes, complete with pot and potting compost.

To get hippeastrums to flower in subsequent years is harder − water and feed until early autumn, then gradually stop. Move to a cool, frost-free spot and bring into the warmth and resume watering when new growth appears in spring.

Fireplaces are the main architectural feature that often distinguish living rooms from other rooms in the house. The mantelpiece, especially if mirror-backed, is a good position for a plant, pair of plants or linear landscape, complete with fruit, pine cones, *objets trouvés* or small collections of china or even pebbles. Trailing plants on a mantelpiece can create a pretty waterfall of greenery.

A disused grate is a traditional place for a single, large, specimen fern or substantial group of tough, shade-tolerant houseplants, which can be misted and watered without fear of spillage. Use bricks or inverted pots to raise the level of plants in back of the group, if necessary. Use an old-fashioned, brass surround to define the boundaries of a fireplace 'garden', packing it with plants.

Large inglenook fireplaces can feature hanging baskets of plants suspended, at various heights, from hooks; a pair of hanging baskets can also be suspended from brackets either side of a fireplace. Some modern fireplaces are small and badly proportioned; use a cut-to-fit mirror to block the dark hole and draughts, and display plants in front. Painting the cavity of a disused fireplace white also makes a nicer setting for houseplants than a gloomy black one, and increases available light.

In summer add temporary colour to a fireplace foliage display with begonias, ageratum or fuchsias. For a special occasion, bring in a flowerpot in full flower from the garden or patio, display it in an out-of-use fireplace and return it as soon as possible afterwards.

Televisions are an almost universal feature of living rooms and may have an overbearing presence. Placing a television on a bentwood or other wooden bench or large chair and surrounding it with plants, so it nestles under the huge leaves of Swiss cheese plant (*Monstera deliciosa*), for example, robs it of much of its dominance. On a smaller scale, a television 'sprouting' a cineraria (*Senecio cruentus* hybrids)

Personal retreat

△ A woven wicker, planter-style chair on its own is transformed into a retreat for one by a large, overhanging specimen bamboo. Although the graceful fronds of bamboo – actually an outsized member of the grass family – add a tropical touch, any large, specimen houseplant tree with arching branches would suffice – weeping fig, for example.

Low key

▷ Houseplants, even in a living room, don't have to make a major design statement. In this quietly restful decor, a specimen tree and modest, medium-sized foliage plants add to the cool, green and white of the room. A basket of cut garden foliage provides short-term bulk and interest. Note how the mirror almost doubles the greenery.

Exotica

Cymbidiums, the easiest orchids to grow as houseplants, add dark, exotic emphasis to a dream-like painting and mantelpiece collection of golden sunburst ornaments.

Cymbidiums like high humidity in high temperatures, a cool but frost-free winter rest and, being epiphytic, a free-draining potting compost, with plenty of osmunda fibre. You can buy special orchid pots with extra-large drainage holes; orchid baskets, traditionally made of slatted wood; and special orchid fertilizer, from larger garden centres and specialist suppliers.

Victoriana

Victorian fairings stand guard over a copper planter featuring typical Victorian plants: *Maranta tricolor*, with its herringbone-like variegations, and *Billbergia*, or queen's tears, whose arching sprays of colourful, teardrop-like flowers played to the Victorian penchant for romance and high emotions.

Billbergia is a tough-as-nails bromeliad; *Maranta* requires high humidity, steady warmth and a steady supply of water in the growing season.

or poinsettia (*Euphorbia pulcherrima* hybrids) adds a light-hearted touch. In all these cases, immaculate watering is essential!

Sofas and coffee tables are major items of furniture associated with living rooms. Partner a sofa, desk or armchair with a substantial plant or, for symmetrical formality, have an identical plant either side. Palms with their arching fronds are especially effective, creating a pleasing, semi-enclosed, bower-like effect. A rocking chair, stabilized underneath, makes a homely plant stand, with climbers trained up the rungs of back, and trailers given leave to trail.

A corner coffee table can be the basis of a table-top garden, provided there is another convenient table nearby for the magazines, newspapers, coffee cups and remote control that are part of living-room life.

CHOICE OF CONTAINERS

As with plants, the choice of containers is wide open, but because the living room often houses valuable furniture and carpets, as well as books, electronic equipment and other items vulnerable to water, waterproof *cachepots* tend to be safer, if you water casually,

than flowerpots on saucers. These outer containers can be neutral glazed ceramic or more specifically stylish – Oriental bamboo *cachepots*, for example, or Victorian sprigged ceramic. A few, such as coal scuttles or empty log boxes, have definite living-room, or at least fireplace, connotations. Built-in containers were formerly fashionable but demand total commitment to plants and make for inflexible room layouts.

PLANTS FOR FIREPLACES

Asparagus ferns (*Asparagus* species)
Busy Lizzy (*Impatiens wallerana* hybrids)
False castor oil plant (*Fatsia japonica*)
Fatshedera (x *Fatshedera lizei*)
Grape ivy (*Rhoicissus rhomboidea*)
Hare's foot fern (*Polypodium aureum*)
Kangaroo vine (*Cissus antarctica*)
Mother-in-law's tongue (*Sansevieria trifasciata laurentii*)
Piggyback plant (*Tolmeia menziesii*)
Rose-scented geranium (*Pelargonium graveolens*)
Sword fern (*Nephrolepis exaltata*)
Wandering Jew (*Tradescantia* species and varieties)

Dining Rooms

Dining rooms lie half-way between kitchens and living rooms in terms of use, decor and, often, domestic geography. In many ordinary houses, 'dining area' is a more accurate description, and houseplants can act as living boundaries (see *Room Dividers*, pages 36–37.)

Dining rooms or areas that share the kitchen's informality (see pages 104–107) can display much the same plants and containers: a group of ferns or bromeliads, for example, set in a large stoneware bowl, with walnuts or mixed nuts, in their shells, as a decorative mulch.

Dining rooms or areas that take their cue from a living room can reflect its level of formality: perhaps tiger orchids (*Odonto-glossum* species and hybrids) in a silver punch-bowl or, for formality on a budget, miniature roses clustered in a bed of moss in a white china soufflé dish.

CHOICE OF PLANTS

As in the kitchen, food-related plants are fun but any green or green and white foliage and white flowers add to the over-all atmosphere of restfulness which makes dining a pleasure. Seasonal plants such as snowdrops or marguerites dug up from the garden can be enjoyed and appreciated in an unhurried way as the centrepiece on a dining-room table, where the eye tends to gravitate, and returned to the garden after a few days. Try to choose low-growing houseplants that allow diners to see one another across the table.

Houseplants that match or contrast with table linen are fun: a big pot of ivy, for example, on an ivy-printed tablecloth, or simply miniature roses on a flowery, chintzy one. Houseplants can also repeat the colour theme of the china: blue polyanthus (*Primula polyanthus* hybrids) or grape hyacinths (*Muscari arme-*

Cut and dried

All manner of plants – living, cut, dried and drawn – give this dining room a peaceful, pleasant atmosphere. A *Cymbidium*, almost as attractive out-of-flower as in, takes the window spot, while cut Michaelmas daisies and eucalyptus foliage add temporary verdure and dried love-in-a-mist seedpods provide timeless, unchanging interest.

niacum), for example, filling a traditional, blue-and-white willow pattern soup tureen or gravy boat.

CHOICE OF POSITIONS

The dining-room table is the obvious focal point of the room. Small dining rooms with a central table have a certain inevitable symme-

Desert drama

Hot, arid overtones are emphasized by the choice of desert plants, in this sun-filled dining room. A coconut palm and cut stems of tropical blossom provide vertical interest.

Closer to floor level, a pair of desert cacti and shallow dish of *Echeveria* in flower sit on little stools, which protect the plants from accidental knocks, make them easier to observe and enjoy, and elevate them to the status of honoured guests.

On the screen epi-phytes, technically more tropical than desert, add an airy touch.

All these plants benefit from a spell outdoors in the summer, sunny for the cacti and succulents, and light shade for the epi-phytes and, interestingly, the palm. (Young palms are protected in nature by the shade of other vegetation.)

Herbs and hauteur

△ A classical bust is given a light-hearted touch by a pair of moss baskets containing mixed herbs, including strawberries, chives, thyme and mint.

Although the association of herbs and dining rooms is an obvious one, these herbs are for temporary indoor display only, since the low light levels, heat and dense planting are unsuitable for long-term health and growth.

However, herbs can be easily dug up from the garden and potted up for a special occasion or bought, planted in the moss baskets and then planted out permanently in the garden or windowboxes after-wards.

Here and there

▷ Though it is generally more effective to group houseplants, the scattered approach works well in this spacious dining room. Floors, tables, dressers, benches and buffets are called into service, for long-lived and temporary, seasonal plants.

try and formality, though obviously an old, scrubbed pine table has a different feel from polished mahogany. As well as a centrepiece, consider small individual plants at each setting for a dinner party, if space allows – perhaps a goblet filled with a miniature African violet (*Saintpaulia ionantha* hybrids) or cyclamen (*Cyclamen persicum*) set in moss.

Display plants on sideboards or storage cabinets or on the tops of glass-fronted display cabinets, provided space and access allow. Dining-room windowsills, depending on depth and aspect, can hold a formal row or informal jungle of houseplants and plant-filled corners can also add to the room's formality or informality. The impression you create will depend upon whether the plants are treated identically and symmetrically or not, but make sure circulation is still possible, with the chairs pushed out.

CHOICE OF CONTAINERS

Almost anything goes provided the base won't scratch the table and a felt or baize cloth can prevent this. Moss-lined glass bowls can enhance even the most mundane houseplant or moss-filled spaghetti jars of varying height can create an architectural centrepiece. Using receptacles in the same china pattern as the rest of the service creates a sense of continuity. Motifs on china can also be repeated in the choice of plant: Wedgwood ivy pattern, for example, and ivy. Last, centrepiece containers can be temporary and fun: a flat-based cabbage opened up and its centre removed to hold a small houseplant, for example, or a hollowed out gourd – a scooped-out pumpkin, for example, on a round table, or a huge, scooped-out marrow on a long, narrow one.

For high drama, make a melon basket and fill it with plants instead of fruit salad.

Fantasy landscape

For a memorable dining-table centrepiece, construct this multi-level, half desert, half snowy woodland scene, with or without a bemused bird. Although specific cacti and succulents are listed, any interestingly shaped ones can be used; variegated ivy could be substituted for the plain-leaved species shown; and a round base, for the rectangular one.

Large, rectangular polystyrene base
Polystyrene or dried-flower florist's foam blocks
Glue or wire
Opuntia cacti
Old man cacti (Cephalocereus senilis)
Bishop's-cap cacti (Astrophyllum myriostigma)
Donkey's tail (Sedum morganianum)
Moonstones (Pachyphytum oviferum)
Sphagnum or bun moss
Wire hairpins or U-shaped wires
Trailing ivy stems
Sprigs of eucalyptus
Candles
Bird ornament (optional)
Artificial snow aerosol spray

1 Glue or wire a block or blocks to the base, to create a two-tier foundation, each tier at least as deep as the depth of the pots. Using a smaller block, make a third, upper tier, off centre.

2 Arrange the cacti in their approximate positions, roughly spaced apart on lower and middle tiers. Using the pots as a template, carve holes a little smaller than the diameters and push the pots in as far as the rims.

3 Cover the base, rims and potting compost with a dense, thick layer of moss. Use hairpins or U-shaped wires to hold it in place and pack extra moss where one block meets another, to create a rounded effect.

4 Encircle the base with ivy stems, using hairpins or U-shaped wires to hold them in place. Insert eucalyptus sprigs on the top tier and here and there, filling any gaps.

5 Place the bird on the top tier and spray lightly with 'snow'. Insert the candles, one on each side and one in the middle.

Centre point

Celebrations are an excuse for extravagance and this outrageously beautiful dining-table centrepiece is a perfect example – impractical, perhaps, but memorable.

Fresh bun moss forms the bulk of the display, with cut sprigs of garden foliage including silvery cotton lavender tucked in between, and a small pot of thyme forming a shrubby mound.

White chippings form the frame and visual transition to the white tablecloth, with 'fingers' of chippings extending to individual place settings. Silver-painted pebbles and silver sugared almonds complete the landscape.

Patience and a steady hand is called for, and good timing – made too soon before the event and the cut material is liable to wilt; too close to the event, and pressure and stress may well hinder creativity. If you do attempt a similar display, use a foil or clingfilm base for the central plants, concealing any exposed edges with chippings.

Kitchens

Kitchens range from purely functional spaces for the storage and preparation of food to the heart of the house, for informal entertaining, relaxing and dining as well as cooking. In a compact, galley-type kitchen where space is vital, a token, modest plant may be all that is possible but generous-sized, family-room kitchens can be full of plants. Try to keep heavily used counters and work spaces uncluttered, however, and place hanging plants well away from cupboard doors or shelves to which regular access is required.

Choice of plants

Tough, reliable, long-term houseplants such as cast-iron plant (*Aspidistra elatior*) spider plant (*Chlorophytum comosum* 'Vittatum') and kangaroo vine (*Cissus antarctica*) are as happy in a kitchen as anywhere, but short-term houseplants with berries or fruits such as the bead plant (*Nertera depressa*), ornamental peppers (*Capsicum annuum*), Christmas, Jerusalem or winter cherries (*Solanum capsicastrum*) or the Indian strawberry (*Duchesnea indica*), with its pretty, trailing runners, yellow flowers and strawberry-like fruit have 'foody' connotations, even though their actual berries or fruit are inedible or, in the case of Christmas cherry, poisonous! Most lemon and kumquat trees, however ideal in theory for a kitchen, are too big or temperamental to thrive and fruit in such conditions, though small specimens grown personally from seed always command affection, even if barren for years on end. Some asparagus ferns, such as the sicklethorn fern (*Asparagus falcatus*), produce young shoots that look like edible asparagus, amusing in a kitchen, space permitting. The variegated pineapple plant (*Ananas comosus* 'Variegata'), with its tiny fruit nestling in a rosette of handsome foliage, makes an excellent centrepiece for the kitchen table.

Humidity from the sink and cooker (stove) favours ferns, African violets, Cape primroses (*Streptocarpus* hybrids) and gloxinias (*Sinningia* hybrids), provided temperature remains fairly constant.

Kitchens, like front halls, often lead to the garden and garden plants can provide temporary kitchen colour: in early summer, bedding trays, or flats, of ageratum, petunias, French or African marigolds or tobacco plants can spend a few days on a large kitchen table as a seasonal display, in transit from garden centre to garden; in autumn, buy trays, or flats, of 'Universal' pansies or polyanthus. Use a shallow, rectangular basket to conceal the plastic container. The cost of a tray, or flat, of bedding flowers compares favourably with conventional houseplants and in bright, airy cool conditions, they can cheer up a kitchen for a week or so before they need moving into the garden. For smaller tables, decant one or more plants into a flowerpot. Ornamental cabbages, in various combinations of creamy white, pink, purple and grey-green, are sold individually as winter bedding plants but can also make singularly stunning focal points, displayed in a moss basket as the centrepiece of a kitchen table.

For seasonal sequence, fill a kitchen indoor windowsill with a windowbox planted with spring bulbs such as daffodils, hyacinths or early tulips, followed by pelargoniums and

Cabbages and kings

Ornamental cabbages and kales are popular bedding plants for autumn and winter, when little else provides garden colour. (They are also immensely popular winter fare for pigeons, snails and slugs!)

Indoors, they are temporary plants, but can still be enjoyed for a few days before being transplanted outdoors. Here, with their culinary overtones, they add colour to a monochromatic kitchen, and individual leaves can be removed and shredded to add colour to winter salads.

Kitchen windowsills often end up filled with domestic clutter. Instead, use them as a propagating area for rooting cuttings in glasses or jars of water. Start with scrupulously clean containers and change the water regularly to avoid a buildup of algae – as unappealing in the kitchen as it is in the wild.

Here, newly rooted cuttings include scented-leaved pelargonium, ivy and *Cyperus*. You could also root cuttings of garden plants.

then herbs, potted up from the garden for autumn and winter use.

CHOICE OF POSITIONS

Kitchen windowsills, like bathroom windowsills, are potential linear gardens in miniature, ideal for glass tumblers full of cuttings and, sunny windowsills, for culinary herbs, the consummate kitchen/garden plants (see pages 30–31). Windows themselves can be fitted with equally spaced-out glass shelves or one broad shelf near the top. Hang plant-filled baskets in front of the windows above head height or at varying heights, for a curtain of greenery.

Hanging baskets above a sink benefit from rising steam; hanging baskets, combined with large, floor-level plants, can divide kitchen from dining area, as can open, plant-filled shelves above counters, or shelves suspended from the ceiling on chains. The tops of high-level cupboards and cabinets can also hold plants, provided there is access for watering and the plants can tolerate the rising heat.

Climbers such as grape ivy (*Rhoicissus rhomboidea*) or, for large-scale impact, chestnut vine (*Tetrastigma voinerianum*), with its horse-chestnut-like leaves, can be trained against exposed brick walls, for an outdoor feeling. Tie the climbers to nails in the mortar or fix rigid panels of plastic-coated wire mesh to the brickwork and train the plants to the mesh. A pair of climbers can also be trained up and around a window, as a living frame, or, where a wide archway separates the work space from dining space, around and over the arch.

On kitchen tables used for eating, place houseplants centrally or against a wall or window, in the same way as for dining tables (see pages 98–99) or suspend a hanging plant from the centre of the ceiling above the table.

CHOICE OF CONTAINERS

Containers can be neutral or mirror the nature or decor of the room – a group of small houseplants, for example, *en masse* in a fruit- or vegetable-shaped ceramic container, such as Portuguese glazed ceramic cabbages and cauliflowers, casserole dishes, soup tureens and serving bowls. Small plants can be placed in ceramic tomatoes, originally produced by the famous Austrian firm Royal Beirut but similar, less expensive pieces are also available.

Standing ovation

◁ A cunning tiered stand is used to display houseplants, houseplant cuttings, domestic items and small objets d'art.

The chipping-filled glass cubes that act as *cachepots* for the forced hyacinths and *Cyperus* add a sense of rhythm and coherence.

Space saver

△ Horizontal space in a small kitchen can be too valuable to use for houseplants, in which case wall-hung containers are an alternative. This kitchen scale contains a variegated creeping fig, which benefits from the kitchen's high humidity.

(Lidless tureens and casseroles can often be had cheap in junk shops.)

Small houseplants can be given stability and pzazz, placed in the centre of a large bowl, which is then filled with fruit, concealing the flower pot: in summer, a pyramidal bowl of strawberries, for example, 'spouting' a miniature pink rose. Wrap the flowerpot in foil or clingfilm to prevent excess water dripping into the bowl, and water with care.

French wirework lettuce shakers can hold hanging plants as alternatives to traditional hanging baskets; wirework colanders, on little legs, can be lined with moss and filled with plants. Empty, decorative metal olive-oil tins or old tea caddies make *cachepots* with kitchen connotations. Or simply hang shopping baskets – burlap, woven rope or decorative plastic – on a kitchen wall and fill with trailing or arching plants, padding out the bag with newspaper or dried moss, if necessary.

TIP
Wash the leaves of plants (except African violets) regularly to remove greasy deposits from cooking.

Bedrooms

Relatively little waking time is spent in a bedroom but it is the most personal room in a house and the one in which fantasies, decorative and otherwise, are most freely expressed. Houseplants can reinforce decor and fantasy – austere or luxurious, predatory or feminine – with form, scent and colour, while greenery always adds to the sense of repose so important in a bedroom.

CHOICE OF PLANTS

Any houseplant can be displayed in a bedroom but some types have special relevance. Extra large-leaved plants such as the Swiss cheese plant (*Monstera deliciosa*), Chinese fan palm (*Livistonia chinensis*) and tree philodendrons (*Philodendron bipinnatifidum*, *P. selloum*), for example, can convey the dream-like, jungly quality of a Henri Rousseau painting, especially if they are substantial specimens or clustered with other, similar plants.

Bedrooms kept continually warm are ideal for scented tropical plants such as *Hoya carnosa* and *Stephanotis floribunda*. White- and yellow-flowered forms of the so-called orchid cactus (*Epiphyllum cooperi* and *E.* hybrids) carry heavily scented, huge, almost sinfully showy flowers that open in the evening, when a bedroom is coming into use.

For short-term winter interest with a feminine touch, combine cyclamen, azaleas and polyanthus, all in shades of pink or white, in a toning basket or bowl on a dressing table. In late winter and early spring combine bowls or flowerpots of forced hyacinths and cut hyacinths, or forced and cut narcissi, as a charming *pot et fleur*. In summer display miniature rose bushes in a large, wide bowl filled with rosepetal or rosebud pot-pourri. Equally feminine are orchids; cymbidiums are among the easiest and most reliable to flower and top-quality silk orchids can be tucked among a dense group of foliage houseplants, for fool-proof femininity.

CHOICE OF POSITIONS

Windowsills can hold a collection of small plants, single specimens or, for a formal effect in a large window, a row of climbers such as pink jasmine (*Jasminum polyanthum*), passion-flower (*Passiflora caerulea*) or ornamental potato vine (*Solanum jasminoides* 'Album') trained up tall bamboo tripods.

In small bedrooms a centrally placed double bed often creates a sense of symmetry, which can be emphasized with a pair of tall weeping figs (*Ficus benjamina*) or palms either side of the head of the bed, or one in each corner, canopy style. At the foot of a bed, set out a row of substantial, tree-like houseplants such as the fiddle-leaf fig (*Ficus lyrata*), rubber plant (*Ficus elastica decora*) or even avocado (*Persea americana*).

Table tops, whether dressing table, dresser, desk or bedside table, are obvious locations for plants. Bedside tables are especially appropriate for small, delicate plants, such as grape hyacinths (*Muscari armeniacum*). The top of a little-used hope chest or blanket chest at the end of a bed can also provide space for grouped plants, again pleasant to observe from a lying-down position.

If space allows, fill the deep ledges or the floor beneath dormer windows with houseplants, to make an indoor garden. In converted loft bedrooms, the area beneath a skylight is ideal for specimen plants or plant grouping, provided the general circulation space is unimpaired. Placing a comfortable bedroom chair there, under the arching fronds of a large palm, makes a restful retreat.

CHOICE OF CONTAINERS

Unlike bathrooms, with their connotations of water, and kitchens, with their connotations of food, bedrooms have no particular imagery that is translatable into containers. Anything

is fair game, although obviously the colour scheme and mood of the room can be reflected in the choice of containers. Victorian china bowl-and-jug washstand sets, for example, popular in country-style bedrooms, can set the tone for ceramic *cachepots* in similar floral sprigged or willow-garden designs. The bowl and jug can also contain plants – a collection of variegated, small-leaved ivies, perhaps. Floral wallpaper can be repeated in *cachepots* with hand-painted or transfer-printed floral motifs, or jocular, Sylvac-type *cachepots*, themselves shaped and painted to resemble cacti, arum lilies or other sculptural plants.

Simple solutions

△ This traditional bedroom decor is enhanced by high-level ivy in its wicker basket *cachepot*, and a cluster of plants, including ivy, grape ivy and spider plant, by the window. Glazed ceramic containers protect the furniture from accidental spillage.

Sleeping beauty

(*overleaf*)
Using substantial, arching houseplants such as these striped *Dracaenas* at the head and foot of a bed can be equally effective in more modest bedrooms than this, with simple nightstands or tables replacing the gilded columns. Note the ivy entwining the column, as a Classical finishing touch.

Bathrooms

Bathrooms can be bright and sunny or totally devoid of natural light; generously spacious or confined; steadily warm or cold or wildly fluctuating in temperature; hard and sparsely hygienic or frilly and feminine; and conducive to lingering or the reverse. Most are less extreme variations of the above and in various combinations, with decorative style equally wide ranging.

Conventional bathrooms provide windowsill, floor, shelf and ceiling space as potential houseplant display areas. Such plants are best as large specimens or in tight groups – scattered, small plants are liable to get visually lost among a plethora of cosmetic and medicinal containers. Stability and sensible positioning are important since the smaller the space, the more liable a plant is to get knocked over.

If the toilet is in a separate, small alcove or indeed, in a separate room of its own, the presence of a surrounding, floor-to-ceiling jungle of plants can be most welcome – peaceful and more contemplative than the pile of old magazines often placed there.

Windows

Privacy is paramount in a bathroom and a windowsill full of dense, substantial houseplants or single large houseplant can help provide privacy and help disguise obscured glass, itself a mundane feature of modern life. The common scented-leaf geranium, *Pelargonium fragrans*, is an ideal windowsill specimen plant;

Lovely light

This unusual bathroom, with its rich, Victorian detail, manages to combine large areas of transparent glass with complete privacy, and the houseplants as well as the owners benefit. The occasional high humidity when baths are drawn, and the damping down from occasional splashes are a further bonus for the ferns, palm, philodendron, castor-oil plant and parasol plant.

113

Less is more

◁ A single palm and fern, coupled with cut tulips, add life and colour to this all-white bathroom. Substantial, healthy specimens need no adornment and need less maintenance than masses of smaller plants.

The tulips can be replaced with white roses, lilies, iris, orchids or chrysanthemums, to ring the changes.

Purpose built

▷ A designer bathroom merits designer plants. Here, a purpose-built, permanent planter is filled with the spiky foliage of *Dracaena marginata*, and the elegant, tropical leaves and white, sail-like spathes of the humidity-loving *Spathyphyllum*.

its dense, intricate leaves and well-branched, vigorous growth habit can create a curtain of greenery which will completely fill the rectangular space and provide a pleasant, fresh fragrance.

Arching or trailing plants overspilling a bathroom window can enliven the side elevation of the wall. In windowless bathrooms, fake plants (see pages 28–29) are the best long-term solution and can be extraordinarily dramatic, especially mixed with cut fresh flowers or short-term pot plants.

SHELVES

Plant-filled glass window shelves are welcome in a bathroom, placing plants out of harm's way and creating a potentially large impact with modest-sized, inexpensive raw material.

Trailing plants mixed with upright ones help visually unify the disparate components. Trailing plants can also be positioned on top of a bathroom cabinet or cistern.

You can root cuttings of houseplants such as tradescantia, African lime (*Sparmannia africana*) or begonias in tumblers of water on a bathroom-window shelf. The cuttings look every bit as attractive as young plants and you can enjoy watching their roots form. The water should be keep crystal clear, for the sake of the cuttings and appearance.

The top of the cistern can be used as a shelf, perhaps with a tight row of piggy-back plants (*Tolmeia menziesii*) forming a verdant, horizontal mass. Plants on bathtub corner shelves may be photogenic but can also be easily knocked over!

115

FLOORS AND WALLS

Floor space in a bathroom is usually at a premium but the otherwise 'dead' space either side of a toilet can be filled with vertical plants, and the obligatory lavatory brush well and truly concealed! The umbrella plant (*Cyperus alternifolia*) is a good candidate, or the elegant, tall sicklethorn fern (*Asparagus falcatum*) or ubiquitous weeping fig (*Ficus benjamina*).

If space allows, fix plant pots to a sturdy, plastic-coated wire wall-trellis panel, sold in DIY shops for hanging up towels, soap dishes and other bathroom accessories.

CEILINGS

Bathrooms with high ceilings, especially skylights, can be enhanced with hanging baskets of common houseplants such as ivy, Boston fern (*Nephrolepis exaltata* varieties), mother-of-thousands (*Saxifraga stolonifera* 'Tricolor'), spider plant (*Chlorophytum comosum* 'Vittatum') and epiphytes such as cymbidium orchids.

CHOICE OF PLANTS

Long-term foliage plants tend to perform better than long-term flowering ones in bathrooms, with high humidity (even from damp towels!) and medium-to-low light levels favouring ferns and other thin-leaved plants. These can make a good backdrop for short-term flowering plants such as cyclamen or fragrant, forced hyacinths or 'Paperwhite' narcissi in winter, brought into the bathroom when just coming into bloom. The cool temperatures prolong the display period and natural floral fragrance is a welcome alternative to the patently artificial scent of room fresheners and many pot-pourris.

In spring, bring in pots of forced, scented Easter lilies (*Lilium longiflorum*); in summer, introduce the equally fragrant Madonna lilies (*Lilium candidum*) or ginger lilies (*Hedychium* species) just as they are about to flower and then return them to the garden when finished

– in a cool bathroom, flowering can last two or more weeks.

African violets (*Saintpaulia* varieties and hybrids) and the related Cape primroses (*Streptocarpus* hybrids) are exceptions to the rule, as these are long-term flowering plants that can thrive in warm, humid, reasonably well-lit bathrooms.

Bathrooms are also ideal for *pot et fleur* arrangements (see pages 82–87), using cut fresh or fake flowers with foliage plants; you can also used dried flowers though high humidity can cause them to rot.

Cool, bright or medium-bright bathrooms can be treated as an extension of the garden in winter, housing not-quite hardy, containerized evergreen shrubs such as plain or variegated forms of myrtle (*Myrtus communis*), fatsia (*Fatsia japonica*) or fatshedera (*x Fatshedera lizei*). For instant, bright impact, buy a spotted laurel (*Aucuba japonica*) for a cool, bright bathroom – the Victorians used them as greenhouse and houseplants as well as outside. Not-quite hardy garden-pond plants such as water hyacinth (*Eichornia crassipes*) or the delicate fairy moss (*Azolla caroliniana*) can also overwinter in an aquarium or glass bowl

Semi-private

◁ Houseplants filling bathroom windows act as curtains, the opacity depending on the density of the foliage and the spacing between plants. Here, two rows of small plants create a semi-private effect, fine for a fully private window.

Little landscape

▷ Maidenhair ferns, lilies in an attractive twig cachepot and a standard weeping fig comprise a sink-side landscape, again benefitting from the high humidity normally found in a bathroom.

in a bathroom, the plants fascinating in their unexpectedness and the water a visual reference to the purpose of the room. Continuing the watery theme, clear-glass, water-filled cylinders or bowls can contain lacy, tropical aquarium plants, purchased from tropical fish specialists and the ultimate bathroom plants!

CHOICE OF CONTAINERS

Glazed ceramic containers provide stabilizing weight and, in ceramic tiled bathrooms, a sense of continuity. *Cachepot* containers with-overtones of ablution include shaving mugs and, where space allows, Victorian washstand jug and bowl sets. Shell motifs are always suitable for a bathroom, and a small fern growing in a conch shell, real or ceramic, is a pretty finishing touch.

TIP

Wash leaves regularly to remove deposits of talcum powder, hairspray and deodorant spray.

PLANTS FOR WELL-LIT BATHROOMS
African violet (*Saintpaulia* varieties)
Cape primrose (*Streptocarpus* hybrids)
Devil's ivy (*Scindapsus aureus*)
Italian bellflower (*Campanula isophylla*)
Ivy (variegated *Hedera helix* varieties)*
Jasmine (*Jasminum polyanthum*)*
Kangaroo vine (*Cissus antarctica*)*
Piggyback plant (*Tolmeia menziesii*)*
Scented-leaved geranium (*Pelargonium fragrans*)*
Umbrella plant (*Cyperus alternifolia*)*
Weeping fig (*Ficus benjamina*)

*tolerates low temperatures

PLANTS FOR SHADY BATHROOMS
Asparagus ferns (*Asparagus* species)*
Bird's-nest fern (*Asplenium nidus-avis*)
Button fern (*Pellaea rotundifolia*)
Cast-iron plant (*Aspidistra elatior*)*
Chinese evergreen (*Aglaonema* species)
Creeping fig (*Ficus pumila*)
Grape ivy (*Rhoicissus rhomboides*)
Holly fern (*Cyrtomium falcatum*)*
Ivy (plain-leaved *Hedera helix* varieties)*
Maidenhair fern (*Adiantum capillus-veneris*)
Net leaf (*Fittonia* species)
Piggyback plant (*Tolmeia menziesii*)*
Sweetheart plant (*Philodrendron scandens*)
Umbrella plant (*Cyperus alternifolia*)*

Conservatories

Traditional conservatories were used to display ornamental plants, with people in the role of transient admirers whose comfort came secondary. Today, however, many conservatories, especially prefabricated or modular types, are fully carpeted, fully heated extensions of the living or dining space, with plants incidental, if included at all. This seems a shame, as conservatories, with their high light levels and less directional light, can provide ideal growing conditions for plants and, if used at night, benefit from a sense of enclosure and privacy that large or grouped plants provide. Of all rooms conservatories offer the opportunity to create an environment balanced between plants and people.

THE CHOICE OF POSITIONS

Plants in conservatories furnished as living rooms or dining rooms can be chosen and placed as such (see pages 90–97 and 98–103). In conservatories in which plants play a major role, the difference is mostly a matter of degree and proportion. Instead of three discreet plants in a living-room corner, a potted, floor-level forest can be created of a dozen or more intermingling plants, with a path through to a table or comfortable seat. Traditional, permanent, floor-level or raised soil perimeter planting beds dispense with the need for containers altogether and provide the grounds for genuine plant communities.

Climbing plants can be trained up walls and along wires or rafters, creating a ceiling or grotto of greenery, perhaps punctuated with hanging baskets. In unheated or slightly heated, transparent-roofed conservatories, deciduous climbers such as grape vines allow maximum light in in winter, when needed, and provide leafy shade in summer.

Most conservatories have one solid wall, to which can be fixed plant shelves at various levels, trellises, plastic-coated wire-mesh panels or wires and vine eyes, to support climbers. Fanciful Victorian or reproduction wirework tiered plant stands are ideal, as are tiered, chrome and glass display shelves.

THE CHOICE OF PLANTS

A fully heated conservatory is ideal for indoor trees: the finger-leaved umbrella tree (*Schefflera actinophylla*) and parasol plant (*Heptapleurum arboricola*), and the tree philodendron (*Philodendron bipinnatifidum*). In cooler conservatories, kangaroo thorn (*Acacia armata*), mimosa (*Acacia dealbata*) and oleander (*Nerium oleander*) can thrive.

Climbers normally considered compact can reach huge size in a conservatory; ivy-leaved geraniums (*Pelargonium peltatum* hybrids), for example, can grow 1.8 m (6 ft) or more in length, the wand-like stems of the sky-blue flowered Cape leadwort (*Plumbago auriculata*) 3m (10ft) or more and the normally diminutive creeping fig (*Ficus pumila*), can cover an entire wall.

You can treat an unheated or cool conservatory as an extension of the garden, with pots of bulbs such as glory-of-the-snow (*Chiono-*

Indoor, outdoor

A magnificent grape vine dominates this comfortably furnished conservatory, which is used as an extra living room for much of the year.

As is shown here, grapevines for conservatories are traditionally planted outdoors for maximum exposure to seasonal temperature changes and their stems trained indoors, through a hole in the wall or foundations, to make maximum use of solar gain.

Because they are deciduous, vines allow light in during the colder months, when light levels are low, and their leaves provide welcome shade in the hot months.

In cool temperate climates, go for sweet-flavoured dessert varieties such as the shy-fruiting muscats or the popular and traditional 'Black Hamburgh'.

Grape vines need cool winter conditions to induce dormancy, so winter heating can be kept to a minimum or, in the case of hardy varieties such as 'Black Hamburgh', dispensed with entirely.

Indoor garden

A plethora of foliage plants, including ferns, ivies and out-of-flower jasmine, are punctuated with occasional flowers – white campanulas, and pelargoniums, streptocarpus and gloxinias in shades of pink and purple. The floral tablecloth is seasonless, providing flowers, albeit two-dimensional, all year round.

A sense of proportion

The relative proportion of conservatory space devoted to plants, as opposed to furniture or circulation space, is a matter of personal taste and committment – how much time you are prepared to give to plant maintenance. Here, a sweetly scented, double pink oleander tree dominates the smaller plants, including maidenhair ferns, streptocarpus, palm, African violets, weeping figs and the exotic, pink-flowered medinella.

Note the formal pair of ceiling-hung sweetheart vines, and the ceramic swans containing mind-your-own-business, *Soleirolia soleirolii*.

The table centrepiece, of garden pinks and variegated *Sedum sieboldii*, helps to create a continuity between conservatory and garden, as does the tile flooring.

doxa luciliae), annuals such as love-in-a-mist (*Nigella damascena*) and alpine plants such as alpine pink (*Dianthus alpinus*) or gentian (*Gentiana verna*), flowering early and with blooms unblemished by weather.

Fragrant plants such as pink jasmine (*Jasminum polyanthum*) are valuable since still, warm conservatory air concentrates and intensifies scent, which also wafts indoors when the connecting door is opened.

Last, a conservatory is a good home for flamboyant fakes, particularly if they are placed at high or roof level, so that a detailed examination of them is not possible.

THE CHOICE OF CONTAINERS

You can play it either way. For a garden look, you can use terracotta or stone or reconstituted stone containers, which are ideal for brick, reconstituted stone or concrete-slab-paved conservatory floors. You could also successfully use these on green carpeted floors, with their poetic reference to lawns. If the conservatory is furnished as an indoor room, you can use the most delicate and refined containers or *cachepots*, to match. Bamboo and wicker furniture often feature in conservatories, and *cachepots* to match can reflect their informal simplicity.

123

Appendix

Buying the best

Try to use sources with a high volume and rapid turnover, with 'sell by' or 'display until' labels. (Large volume and rapid turnover usually mean low prices.) Multiple stores and garden centres, and nurseries specializing in one type of houseplant such as cacti have their reputations on the line and tend to offer only top quality stock. If unsure about which plant to buy, ask a member of staff, and ask why he or she has chosen that particular one

Houseplants on market stalls or pavements outside shops may have been exposed to extremes of temperature and wind, according to season, and car fumes and dust. On the other hand, houseplants in hot, corner shops may be on their last legs and houseplants encased in clear cellophane may be more or less held together by it; discreetly unwrap the plant to check on its health and shape and re-wrap afterwards. Very gently shaking a plant reveals any flowers or leaves that would have fallen off anyway, as soon as you got it home.

Go for compact plants with close-jointed growth, dense, healthy foliage, according to type and, if flowering, a few open flowers and plenty of buds showing colour. Very immature, green buds may fail to open altogether and those with flowers fully open have used up much of their display life. If you are buying daisy-like plants – single chrysanthemums, for example, or cinerarias – tight, velvety centres are signs of youth; fluffy centres, dusty with pollen, are signs of old age, as are translucent petals, especially with lilies, or dry, curled edges, especially with flower spathes such as arum lily or painter's palette.

A slimy pot or potting compost surface; soggy or bone-dry potting compost; roots growing out of the drainage hole; or a shrunken rootball smaller than the pot are danger signs. Check under the leaves and any soft growing tips for signs of greenfly. If the plant is meant to be clothed in foliage to the base, make sure it is, and avoid plants with yellow, brown-edged, bruised or wilted leaves. Unless the character of the plant is asymmetrical – some bonsai, for example, or mature, multi-headed specimens of the Madagascar dragon tree (*Dracaena marginata*) – try to choose a well balanced plant, evenly developed on all sides.

The right spot for the right plant

Follow plant care labels but generally, thin, delicate leaves such as maidenhair fern and creeping fig prefer semi-shade and humidity; the thicker or tougher the leaf, the more it tolerates sun and dry atmosphere. (Grey-, silver-, waxy- and woolly-leaved plants need sun to maintain those qualities.) No plant likes deep shade – as a rough guide, insufficient natural light to read by.

Colourful, variegated leaves such as coleus and crotons need plenty of light to colour well and most plants need good light to form flowers. Houseplants bought in flower, however, flower virtually anywhere.

No plant likes draughts from doors, windows or air conditioners, coal or gas fumes or excess heat – above a refrigerator, for example. Windowsills over radiators can be hell for houseplants, with draughts from the windows and dry rising heat from the radiator.

Food, water, temperature and air

Food, water and heat are interrelated. Houseplants in active growth – usually but not always from spring until autumn, when temperatures are high – need regular feeds with liquid fertilizer, granules or slow-release fertilizer tablets, according to the manufacturer's instructions. (Newly bought houseplants have a month's worth of nutrients in peat-based potting compost, six to eight weeks' worth in loam-based.) The quicker the plant's natural growth, the more nutrients are needed; overfeeding, however, can cause weak, lanky growth and, in extremis, death.

Plants generally need water when they need food, and in similar proportions – more in growth and flower than when dormant, and more in warm weather than in cold. (Cycla-men is an obvious exception, its growth cycle reflecting its Persian origins, where the blistering summer is a period of natural dormancy.) Erratic supplies of water or food may cause buds, flowers or fruit to drop.

More houseplants are killed by overwatering than any other cause; the same plants – silver-, grey-, woolly- or waxy-leaved – that need maximum sunlight are especially vulnerable to overwatering. Once a week is enough for most houseplants, less when dormant; thoroughly moisten but don't saturate the potting compost. If, however, peat-based potting compost, used by the vast majority of growers, dries out completely, submerge the pot in a sinkful of water until bubbles stop rising from the potting compost. Water plants such as umbrella plant (*Cyperus alternifolius*) and variegated miniature sweet flag (*Acorus gramineus* 'Variegatus') are exceptions, needing

continually saturated potting compost and are best set in bowls of water.

Most popular houseplants, especially Cool Temperate climate garden-origin plants such as polyanthus, jasmine, ivy, forced hyacinths and tulips, miniature roses and azaleas, like temperatures that roughly follow the Cool Temperate climate cycle: cool late autumns, winters and early springs, and cooler nights than days. Tropical houseplants such as stephanotis, crotons and angel's wings need steady warmth, day and night, all year round.

Except for grey-, silver-, waxy- and woolly-leaved plants, most plants like increased humidity in increased temperatures, so mist spray in hot weather. Fresh air is also important all year round, to strengthen the plant and help prevent fungal and other diseases, but avoid direct draughts.

SEASONAL VARIATIONS

In Cool Temperate climates, most plants benefit from bright sun in winter, when light levels are low, but except for cacti, succulents and zonal pelargoniums, sunny windowsills in summer are also unbearable, with the solar gain from the glass intensifying the heat. Try to remember to move plants towards and away from a source of natural light from season to season. Moving houseplants outdoors for summer is also beneficial.

Central heating creates seasonless climates indoors, which confuse houseplants' natural rhythms. An unheated, sunny spare room is invaluable for overwintering plants such as pelargoniums, jasmine, passionflower, piggyback plant, orange and lemon trees and cacti, which prefer cool periods of dormancy.

TENDER LOVING CARE

Again, follow the guide on the care label. Keep the leaves dusted, wiping them down with a damp cloth from time to time, if practical.

Pruning is not as much a regular requirement for indoor as for outdoor plants because the growth rate is slower. Nonetheless, at the start of the growth season, usually early spring, prune back woody stemmed houseplants that have outgrown their alotted space, and those that have grown lanky over winter. Cut back by ¼ to ⅓ to just above a growth bud, using secateurs or sharp scissors. (Houseplants such as palms, cacti, ferns and bromeliads do not benefit from pruning.)

The start of the growth season is also the time to repot long-term houseplants into fresh potting compost, either in the same pot, or, if outgrown, a pot no more than 5cm(2in) larger in diameter. Exceptions include clivia and most long-term bulbs such as Scarborough lily (*Vallota speciosa*) and blood lily (*Haemanthus* species), which flower best when their roots are crowded, or potbound. If using terracotta pots, place a layer of broken pots or pebbles in the base, to aid drainage; plastic pots do not need 'crocking'. Carefully tease out the old potting compost from the roots, place in the pot to the same depth as before, and fill with fresh potting compost, working it in with your fingers and tapping the pots as you proceed, to ensure that it settles. Water lightly and leave in semi-shade for a few days, for the plant to recover.

Many potentially bushy houseplants such as spotted flowering maple (*Abutilon striatum* 'Thompsonii'), rex begonia, coleus, pelargonium and finger aralia (*Dizygotheca elegantissima*) can be encouraged to branch, forming compact, attractive specimens, by regularly pinching out, or stopping, the growing tips. Use your forefinger and thumb, pinching back to a leaf or growth bud.

Remove faded blooms, or deadhead, to keep a flowering houseplant looking good, prevent unnecessary energy spent on the development of seeds and encourage the production of further flower buds. Use your forefinger and thumb for soft plants, or secateurs or a sharp scissors for tougher ones, cutting back to a leaf, growth bud or, as in the case of polyanthus, to the base. Always remove discoloured, yellow or brown leaves.

WHEN TO SAY GOODBYE

The purpose of a houseplant is to look nice and when it ceases doing so questions are bound to arise. Those that obviously give up the ghost – a waterlogged African violet, for example, with rotten leaf stalks – are easily disposed of but life often exists in a houseplant long after it looks dead. Cyclamen, tuberous-rooted begonias, Italian bellflowers, hippeastrums and caladiums, for example, look dead when flowers and foliage have died back but are in fact dormant. With proper care – usually an extended period of dry, warm conditions – they can be repotted in fresh compost, watered lightly and gradually brought back to life.

Other houseplants such as poinsettia and winter cherry lose visual value once they finish flowering or fruiting but can theoretically be saved for future displays – winter cherry needs cutting back and a dry rest period followed by summer outdoors; poinsettia needs cutting back, a dry rest period, repotting in late spring and 14 hours a day darkness from early autumn for eight weeks. Even 'annuals' such as cineraria, tobacco plant, antirrhinum, cup-and-saucer vine, petunia and verbena are capable of many years' of life, given ideal aftercare. Most people, however, don't want the bother and are quite happy to discard all these houseplants and start again fresh.

With some plants, however, there is an easy way to half-say goodbye. You can discard a lank coleus, wandering Jew, pelargonium or busy Lizzie, for example, but first cut off the top 10–15cm (4–6in) of healthy stems, nip off any flowers and any leaves on the lower third, and insert in potting compost, burying the lower third of stem, to root. Keep the potting compost fairly moist, but on the dry side for the pelargonium.

Index

127